BEHIND THE MASK

THE IAN YOUNG GOALTENDING METHOD

by IAN YOUNG and CHRIS GUDGEON

Polestar Book Publishers acknowledges the ongoing support of The Canada Council, the British Columbia Ministry of Small Business, Tourism and Culture, and the Book Publishing Industry Development Program of the Department of Canadian Heritage.

Cover design by Jim Brennan.
Interior illustrations and diagrams by Jim Brennan.
All goalie photographs by Chris Relke.
Author photograph by Kathy Bellesisles.
Printed and bound in Canada.

Canadian Cataloguing in Publication Data
    Young, Ian, 1946-
    Behind the mask
    ISBN 1-896095-51-8
    1. Hockey—Goalkeeping. 2. Hockey—Coaching. I. Gudgeon, Chris, 1959-
    II. Title
    GV848.76.Y68 1998   796.962'27 C98-910669-1

Library of Congress Catalogue Number: 98-88274

Polestar Book Publishers
P.O. Box 5238, Station B
Victoria, British Columbia
Canada
V8R 6N4
http://mypage.direct.ca/p/polestar/

In the United States:
Polestar Book Publishers
P.O. Box 468
Custer, WA
USA
98240-0468

To Mr. John Humphries, owner, and to the Management, staff and goaltenders of the Oshawa Generals, all of whom have allowed me to learn the art of goaltending. I thank them all for their generosity.

— Ian Young

To Charlie, Tavish and Keating, with love from their Dad.

— Chris Gudgeon

BEHIND THE MASK

PART ONE: MASTERING THE FUNDAMENTALS

1. Positional Play

2. Puck Play

PART TWO: BEYOND THE FUNDAMENTALS

1. Introduction

2. Skill Development Drills

Ian Young, as goalie for the Oshawa Generals.

FOREWORD
by Chris Gudgeon

By now, many hockey fans know the story of Ian Young. The year was 1967, and Ian was playing his final game as a junior. The experts were predicting big things for Ian; he was rated as the top young goalie in the league, and was expected to follow Bobby Orr, his former Oshawa Generals' teammate, to the NHL's Boston Bruins. It was late in the game, and Ian was feeling a little tired. This was in the days before back-up goalies were common, and he'd played virtually every game of the season. All of a sudden, sniper Mickey Redmond bore down on Ian. Redmond wound up and blasted a shot which hit the maskless young goalie square in the eye. When Ian regained consciousness, he'd lost most of the sight in his eye. In an instant, his dreams of NHL stardom disappeared.

But Ian did not give up. He dedicated himself to learning the craft of goaltending, and to passing on his knowledge to other young goalies who shared his dream of making it in the big leagues. In time, Ian has become one of the most respected goaltending coaches in North America, and the list of goalies he's helped on the road to the NHL is impressive: players like Damian Rhodes, Kirk McLean, Jeff Hackett, Peter Sidorkiewicz, Kelly Hrudey and Mike Fountain. Ian also had a shot at the "Bigs," acting as Goaltending Consultant to teams like the Toronto Maple Leafs and the Vancouver Canucks. Through it all, he hasn't lost sight of his goals — he still spends much of his time coaching and encouraging young goalies as they strive to master one of the most demanding roles in sport.

I met Ian in 1992, after hearing Canucks star goalie Kirk McLean sing his praises. As a former goalie myself — albeit one who'd never progressed past midget hockey — I'd been planning a goaltending manual for a couple years. I'd been frustrated by the level of instructional books that were available. There were a few good ones — I'd been a big fan of Jacques Plante's *Goaltending* in my playing days — but even the best were lacking. In particular, I wanted to write a book that could help the minor league coach. At the lower levels, goalies were too often left to just stand around during practice, waiting for a turn to be sitting ducks for the shooters. I wanted to show coaches how they could incorporate goalies into their entire practices, and, at the same time, help their young netminders develop skills.

I told Ian about my idea, and he readily agreed to help me by sharing all his goaltending and coaching secrets. The result was two books: *Behind the Mask*, published in 1992, and *Beyond the Mask*, which came out a year later. These books have been a commercial and critical success — Don Cherry called them the best-written sports manuals he's ever read. Now, we've decided to come out with a revised edition which combines both books into one convenient package. This "new and improved" *Behind the Mask* is still aimed at goalies and their coaches, and promises to build the skill level of even the most experienced goaltenders. Part One offers an overview of the fundamentals: stance, angles and motion. Part Two offers more advanced exercises, designed to increase skills and reflexes, and to take intermediate and advanced goalies to a whole new level.

If you're a goalie, I hope you enjoy this book and that it helps take your game to a brand-new high. If you're a coach, I hope this book helps you understand the art of goaltending a little better, and shows you how to smoothly incorporate goalies into your practices. Good luck to all of you as you chase your hockey dreams, whatever they may be.

FOREWORD
by Ian Young

On the frozen ponds of Scarborough, Ontario, pick-up hockey games were a daily occurrence. With blazing speed and visions of superstardom, we ten year olds transformed the pond into Maple Leaf Gardens or the Montreal Forum. Every one of us knew where the Gondola was, and with each stride we could hear Foster Hewitt's cry, "He shoots... He scores!" It was an exhilarating time — a time when dreams came true.

As a youngster, I was always the one who fell through the ice; I was also always a step or two behind the rest. It didn't make sense. I had on my faithful old Toronto Maple Leafs sweater and sported a pair of Canadian Tire skates (cleverly labeled "NHL"). I had all the tools, yet lagged badly behind in the scoring race: fifty games, no goals. Did Rocket Richard start out this way?

The following year I moved from the pond to the indoor arena. I was assigned to the Knob Hill Aces of the Scarborough Minor Atom League. I remember peering around the dressing room (yes, a real dressing room) before our first game. Not one pair of Canadian Tire skates here, and everyone had a brand new Toronto Maple Leafs sweater. I melted.

As I contemplated slipping out the door into hockey oblivion, fate stepped in. "Quiet, please," Coach Stovall said, and cleared his throat. "We have a problem. Our goaltender from last season wants to play forward this year. Is there anyone in here who would like to play goal?"

My hand rocketed into the air.

"Okay, you," he said, pointing at me, "the big guy at the back."

In a single moment, I went from being the worst scorer in the room to being the best goalie. Look out Leafs, I thought — here I come!

While my goalie career began on impulse, I was lucky to have some natural ability and fairly good reflexes. I progressed through the minor hockey ranks. Eventually I wound up on the Oshawa Generals, playing alongside the likes of Bobby Orr and Wayne Cashman. By my final year of Junior, the Boston Bruins had approached me: my NHL dreams were coming true. But it all ended suddenly. A slapshot hit me in the face (those, of course, were the days before most goalies wore masks). The bones above and below my eye were shattered, and I was left with four percent peripheral vision.

In a way, you could say it was a blessing in disguise. Because of the injury, I was forced to think about the game of hockey for the first time in my life. I had learned to play goal by trial and error, success and failure. At no time did I have a real goaltender coach. Now, blind in one eye, I had to re-evaluate myself. I realized that if I wanted to stay involved with the game I loved, I would have to learn it inside-out.

I wish I could say that today, twenty-five years later, young goalies are better trained than I was. But I'm disappointed by the lack of goaltending instruction at the minor league level, and the incorrect or inadequate information that makes its way to the developing goaltender. Coaches are not to be blamed. Those who spend their mornings and free time down at the rink are certainly committed to helping their players. But it is not enough to say: "Stay on your feet"; "Watch those rebounds"; "Cut the angles." This manual gives you the tools to be an effective goaltender or goaltending coach.

My story does have a happy ending. As Assistant Coach for the Junior Oshawa Generals, I've watched numerous young men develop into NHL standouts. Kirk McLean, Peter Sidorkiewicz, Jeff Hackett and Mike Fountain — the top goalie chosen in the 1992 NHL Entry Draft — all came out of the Generals' system. Recently, I've made it to the big leagues. I've worked as a Goaltending Consultant with the Toronto Maple Leafs, Vancouver Canucks and New York Islanders.

It's been a strange trip from Scarborough's ponds to Maple Leaf Gardens, but I guess in a way my childhood dreams have finally come true. I hope that I can pass on what I've learned to you, the coach. Now, I won't make any outlandish claims, but I will make one promise: the information in this book will help you become a more effective coach, and allow you to contribute to the sound, fundamental play of the young goalies you work with. And maybe someday, with your help, another ten-year-old's dream will come true.

Good luck!

INTRODUCTION
Seeing Through the Eyes of the Goaltender

Minor league coaches are the forgotten heroes of hockey. You are the ones behind the bench at 5:30 on a Saturday morning, a lukewarm coffee in your hand, trying to instill some order into your Pee Wee team.

We hope that this manual will make your job easier. It's a practical introduction to the fundamentals of goaltending. Look for:

A philosophy of goaltending: this answers the question "Why?"

A description of the fundamentals: this answers the question "What?"

Training tips, team drills and individual exercised to improve and build skills: this answers the question "How?"

The tools for evaluating a goalie's performance and development: this answers the question, "What the heck am I doing at the rink at 5:30 in the morning?"

Our second aim is much more radical. We are asking people to rethink the role of the goalie in hockey today. In no team sport is there a less integrated player than the hockey goalie. He or she is always looked upon as something of an oddball — an outsider looking in.

Too often, we coaches conduct practice almost oblivious to the needs of our goalies. They become the shooting target of other players at the end of a drill. Defensive players practice in pairs; forwards practice as a line; but goalies are left on their own. This sends a false message to goalies: "You are alone."

Perhaps the odd-person-out approach to goalies was once appropriate. But the game of hockey has changed in the last twenty years. The play is much faster and harder; more than ever, hockey is a "team" effort. In reality, goalies are part of a team. They are rarely alone; even on a breakaway or penalty shot, goalies do not bear sole responsibility. Only because of team breakdown does a goalie wind up in a one-on-one situation with a shooter. Today's top goalies skate, stickhandle, pass and shoot as well as anyone. They can even chip in the odd goal, as Ron Hextall demonstrated.

HOW TO USE THIS MANUAL

Behind The Mask is a comprehensive program designed to help the minor league coach to "see through the eyes of a goaltender."

Although we particularly recommend this manual for coaches of players between ten and fourteen years old, every coach and goalie can benefit. As a matter of fact, even with advanced goalies it's a good idea to return to the ideas and exercises in this book — particularly those in Part Two, "Beyond the Fundamentals" — to ensure that your goalies remain sound.

This coach's manual is very simple to use. We've broken into two parts: Part One, which explains the fundamentals of goaltending; and Part Two, which takes the goalie beyond the fundamentals with a series of drills designed to engage the entire team. The fundamentals are broken down into two concepts: positional play and puck play. The first part explains how a goalie prepares for a shot; the second part explains how a goalie reacts to a shot. Skills are presented progressively, in the same order that you should present them to your young goalies. The drills in Part Two concentrate on specific skills and game situations. They are meant to be used over and over again in practices to ensure that goalies build upon the basic skills and take their game to whole new level.

Don't try to memorize the whole book, or even a single section. We've broken everything down into its simplest parts. You only need review a couple of pages before a practice.

Also, coaches say that often they don't have time to work with their goalies. With twenty skaters on a team, and ice time at a premium, how can you devote practice time to one player? Whenever possible, we give you team drills, or have suggested how you can work on a goalie's specific problem without disrupting the flow of your practice'

This is not a coffee-table book. We've tried to make it as practical and "user-friendly" as possible. We'd be happy if you threw it in your hockey bag along with your skates and gloves. We'd also appreciate any suggestions you might have to help make the next edition even better.

HOW YOUNG ATHLETES LEARN

The role of the minor league coach is first and foremost that of teacher. But it's not just "what" you teach that's important, you also need to think of "how" you teach. To be an effective coach it's important to understand how young people learn sports skills, and how you can help enhance this learning process.

Young people learn a little bit at a time. They need to have complicated ideas broken down into smaller parts. They need to have concepts repeated over and over again, before those concepts become "internalized" or second nature. We will help you by focusing on the fundamentals of the game and reducing those skills to their smallest parts.

The younger or more inexperienced your goalie is, the less complicated your approach should be. With some, you may never move past the first chapter. Don't consider this a failure. This is in fact a personal victory; you have resisted the temptation to become impatient. Nothing is more important to a goalie's development that a sound understanding of the fundamentals.

TEACHING METHODS

The problem with trying to teach any skill is that you have very little control over what information makes its way into the learner's brain. There are several ways you can impart your knowledge and each has its own strengths and limitations.

Practice

"Practice makes perfect." True, but the problem is that practice also makes imperfect. If someone practices something the wrong way, at some point they have to unlearn and start over again. It is always easier to learn something right the first time.

It's helpful to not over-practice in a session. It's as effective to work on something a little bit every day as it is to work on something in one big chunk. Also, it's easier to keep kids interested if you don't overdo the practice session.

Verbal Instructions

Many coaches complain that the kids they work with "never seem to listen." Unfortunately, most of us put too great an emphasis on verbal instructions. Don't get frustrated if you find yourself repeating the same instructions over and over again. Think of yourself as the voice in the child's head: the child needs to hear this voice many times before it becomes internalized.

Pictures, Videos and Demonstrations

It's true — pictures are worth a thousand words. Children will often learn more by looking at a picture of a task than by hearing someone describe that task. Of particular importance are pictures that break a task down into several steps. Encourage your goalies to read picture books on the game, and even watch hockey videos.

Nothing beats a live demonstration for "explaining" a skill. If as a coach you can't do it yourself, why not invite an older goalie to your practice to demonstrate some moves? And again, encourage your players to go to live hockey games at all levels. Children learn a lot by watching people they look up to. As a matter of fact, watching others play the sport and replaying their moves in the imagination is one of the most effective ways your goalies will learn.

Whenever possible (and we've tried to help you when we can), use a concrete example to explain your ideas. Remember that concepts which seem simple to you may be beyond the intellectual grasp of a young player.

Feedback

For example, rather than praising a player with a simple "good game," try giving feedback that relates the details of a specific situation. Your goalie needs to hear very specific information: "You stayed on your feet and maintained eye contact on the puck throughout that scramble at the end of the period, and that allowed you to react in time to make the save."

Throughout this book, watch for the Skill Checklists — simple tools that help the coach offer effective feedback to goalies.

COACHING PHILOSOPHY

When coaching children, your emphasis should always be on the intrinsic pleasure of team competition. Think back to your own childhood, to the hours spent on the pond, street or lacrosse box. You went voluntarily, with little regard for winning; you just wanted to play. The Atom or Pee Wee coach whose focus is winning — who benches players, screams at them, who pulls his goalie, or sends "the best players" out for a power play — is sadly misplaced.

Focusing on the intrinsic pleasure of "playing" hockey makes the coach's job easier. There is no greater motivation than encouraging children to participate in something they like doing.

This is not to say that children cannot face challenges or should not work to improve themselves as players. We encourage coaches to push their players to strive beyond their current ability. However, the ultimate goal is not "work hard and the team will win," or "do as I say and some day you'll make the NHL." The fact is that just by participating and being allowed to participate, children will build their skills. The ultimate goal is that young players recognize the sheer joy they get from playing hockey.

PART ONE:
MASTERING THE FUNDAMENTALS

Kirk McLean, guarding his net.

1. POSITIONAL PLAY

ESTABLISHING POSITION TO DEFEND THE NET

INTRODUCTION: The Fundamentals of Goaltending

A goalie's job is to keep the puck out of the net, right? Well…sort of. But that statement is a little unrealistic. No goalie can be expected to stop every single shot (although there's no harm in trying). A more realistic, and less daunting, statement would be helpful. Something like: The goalie's job is to defend the net. Goalies don't have to stop everything; they do have to try and maximize their potential to stop everything.

Goalies are best able to defend the net when they are in position. Positional play is the most important aspect of goaltending. The good news is that positional play is easy to learn. That's not to say that goalies don't have to work hard — you bet they do. But the truth is that the ideas behind positional play are straightforward, simple to teach and fairly easy to learn. Over the next few pages, we'll cover the seven rudiments of positional play. We've broken this section into bite-sized chunks so your brain won't overload. Just take it one rudiment at a time.

To begin, let's look at the three fundamentals of defensive position:

1. Stance
2. Angles
3. Motion

These elements are progressive: the most basic is stance; angles is more advanced; and motion is the most sophisticated. A coach should make sure a goalie can perform well at one level before moving on to the next. We've included several evaluation sheets to help you determine your goalie's progress.

After goalies have mastered the fundamentals of defensive position, we'll look at three more fundamentals designed to help goalies establish position in the net:

4. Establishing the Goalie-Net Relationship
5. Telescoping
6. Taking Position

SECTION 1:
THE FUNDAMENTALS OF DEFENSIVE POSITION

Fundamental #1

STANCE: THE BASIC ELEMENT

THEORY

"Stance" refers to the way goalies position their bodies in anticipation of a shot. An effective stance:
• Feels comfortable to goalies.
• Allows goaltenders to maintain proper balance.
• Covers a maximum area of the net.
• Allows goalies to move with the least amount of effort.

DESCRIPTION

A common myth is that goalies have to keep their legs together. This is not so. The ideal stance is with knees together, slightly bent, and feet apart. This produces an inverted "V" stance. This means that there is a slight opening at the "Five-Hole," the space between a goalie's ankles. The amount of space in the Five-Hole is up to each goalie: he or she must find a spot that feels natural.

Key Point: Knees together, slightly bent, and feet apart.

To maintain proper balance, a goalie crouches forward slightly, so that the line of body weight flows directly from the shoulders to the bent knees. The head is held up. In the proper stance, the goaltender looks something like a knock-kneed swimmer ready to start a race.

Key Points: Shoulders line up with knees; head is up.

Goalies should put their weight on the balls of their feet. A goalie who puts weight on the front of the skate is leaning too far forward and is off balance. A goalie who puts weight on the heel is either leaning too far back or standing too straight. In either case, mobility and balance suffer.

Key Point: Weight on the balls of the feet.

The two gloves — the catching glove or trapper, and the stick glove or blocker — should be kept at knee level, just above the leg pads. At all times, the trapper must remain open. Many young players become so involved in the play that they forget about the trapper and let it drop in front of them. Why have gloves in front protecting your pads? Protect the open net!

Key Point: Keep gloves at knee level, trapper open.

A goalie should hold the stick with the blocker hand. The hand fits snugly over the arch on the shaft of the stick, with the index finger on the front side and the rest of the fingers grabbing the stick. The stick should be in front of the goalie's feet, with the blade flat on the surface of the ice.

Key Point: Always keep the blade flat on the ice.

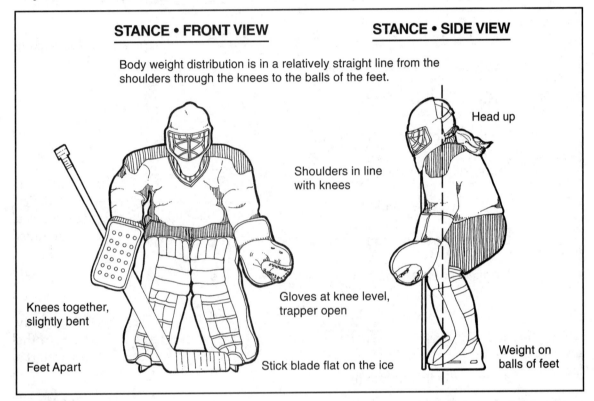

STANCE • FRONT VIEW   **STANCE • SIDE VIEW**

Body weight distribution is in a relatively straight line from the shoulders through the knees to the balls of the feet.

Head up

Shoulders in line with knees

Knees together, slightly bent

Gloves at knee level, trapper open

Feet Apart

Stick blade flat on the ice

Weight on balls of feet

COACHING TIPS

You don't have to spend your entire practice session trying to correct your goalie's stance. Many goalies have just a couple of problems, upon which they should focus during a practice or game. Tell the goalies specifically what you want to concentrate on at the start of a session, and immediately afterwards offer feedback. We encourage you to fill out a Stance Checklist (you could make photocopies of page 20) for your goalies after every game or practice. Even the most advanced goalie can use occasional attention to stance.

If you encounter a very young or inexperienced goalie, work on the stance a point at a time. Explain the general purpose of the stance — "to block as much of the net as possible" — then work on it point by point. Again, this does not mean that you devote an entire practice to whether or not a goalie's knees are together. Explain the point at the start of the practice or game. Offer some feedback, if possible, during the session. At the end of the session, briefly go over the point again with the goalie.

CHECKLIST
Stance

Knees together	Yes	No
Feet apart	Yes	No
Knees slightly bent	Yes	No
Shoulders in line with knees	Yes	No
Head up	Yes	No
Leaning too far forward	Yes	No
Standing too straight	Yes	No
Gloves at knee level	Yes	No
Gloves just above the leg pads	Yes	No
Trapper open all the time	Yes	No
Hand over arch of stick all the time	Yes	No
Stick in front	Yes	No
Stick blade flat on the ice	Yes	No
Did the goalie feel comfortable?	Yes	No

Fundamental #2

ANGLES: THE INTERMEDIATE ELEMENT

There are three aspects to angles:
- *Simple Angles*: the puck as it relates to the centre of the net.
- *Telescoping*: how goalies move forward and backward, while retaining angle.
- *Goalie-Net Relationship*: how goalies establish their position in relation to the net.
    Right now, concentrate on the first aspect, "simple angles." We will pick up "telescoping" and "goalie-net relationship" later.

THEORY

The term "angles" is appropriate, because this is basically a geometric concept. By repositioning themselves in line with the shooter, goalies increase the amount of net they cover. This is what's meant by the term "cutting down the angle." You will find that many goalies have a hard time with this element, so take it one step at a time.

DESCRIPTION

Draw an imaginary line from the centre of the goal line to where the puck is positioned when the shot is taken. The goalie should be facing the shooter, with this imaginary line running through the very centre of the goalie's Five-Hole.

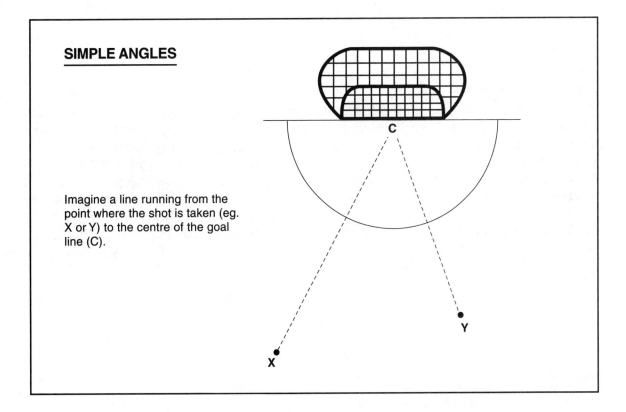

SIMPLE ANGLES

Imagine a line running from the point where the shot is taken (eg. X or Y) to the centre of the goal line (C).

COACHING TIPS

The problem with angles is that you are trying to teach an abstract idea that may be beyond the grasp of your goalie. Demonstrate on a chalkboard or in some other concrete way.

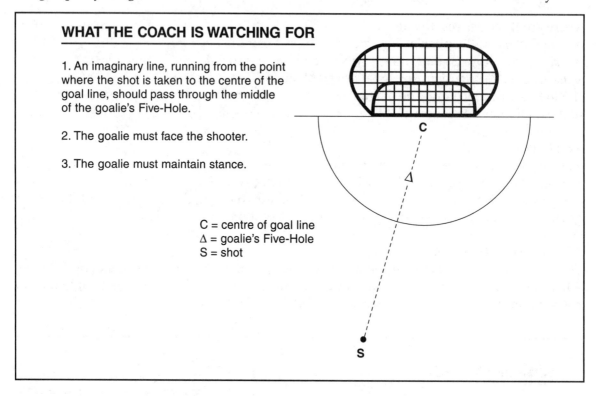

WHAT THE COACH IS WATCHING FOR

1. An imaginary line, running from the point where the shot is taken to the centre of the goal line, should pass through the middle of the goalie's Five-Hole.

2. The goalie must face the shooter.

3. The goalie must maintain stance.

C = centre of goal line
Δ = goalie's Five-Hole
S = shot

TRAINING EXERCISE

An ideal time to work on angles is during shooting practice or the goalie warm-up before a game. It's important that the shooters be stationary and give the goalie time to get into position. To repeat: the shooter should be stationary and the goalie must have time to figure out the proper angle. *The only way goalies will learn about angles is if they are allowed to practice this difficult idea properly.* If goalies do not have time to set up, they are only practicing poor angle play. With more advanced goalies, the set-up time between shooters can be shortened.

It is helpful for the coach to crouch down behind the net to talk the goalie into a proper angle, although you don't want the goalie to become dependent on you. The bottom line is to "be patient." It may take years for a goalie to develop a full understanding of angles.

A NOTE ON SKATING:
Making Motion Possible

Before we look at motion, the last element in positional play, we need to look at the skill that makes motion possible: skating.

A common mistake minor league coaches make is designating their worst skater as goalie. Many coaches think that goalies don't have to work as hard as the other skaters in team skating drills. "Just try to keep up," we tell them. The truth is that goalies must be excellent skaters. They are constantly moving forward, backward, and from side to side in an effort to maintain position. *At all times include the goalies in your skating drills.*

For the most part, goalies skate in the same way as any other player. However, there are situations when they use a unique skating style:
- when moving forward out of the net to cover an angle;
- when moving back into the net to maintain the angle.

When goalies move forward or backward to cover the play, they must do so with a minimum of residual movement. The "power" comes from the feet and ankles. Goalies moving forward do not move their knees or shoulders. Goalies moving backwards do not wiggle their backsides. The important point is that goalies must maintain stance and angle while following the play. A forward and backward motion should be a smooth glide. Too much movement from the leg, knee, backside or shoulder disrupts position and stance.

LATERAL MOVEMENT
Goalies can use two types of skating styles for skating from side to side: the shuffle and the T-Push. The *shuffle* is the most common method, and it requires the least amount of speed. It's used when the puck is away from the net and quick lateral movement isn't required. When puck carriers move in deep towards the net, we recommend goalies use the T-Push. It produces a much smoother motion, and does not open up the Five-Hole.

Shuffle
Starting from the basic stance, and facing the shooter, the goalie who wants to move to the right moves the right foot about shoulder-width distance, then brings the left foot over to the right foot. The reverse happens when the goalie desires to move to the left. This series of moves is the shuffle.

Note: with each step of the shuffle, the Five-Hole opens wide. This, plus the movement's lack of speed, are the two reasons why the shuffle shouldn't be used when the puck is in close.

T-Push
The goalie points the outside skate in the direction he or she wants to move (forming a "t" with the two skates), then pushes with the outside knee to rest against the inside knee. This turns the outside leg pad to better cover the Five-Hole. The T-Push is simpler than it sounds. Let's run through it again.

THE T-PUSH

1. This goalie wants to move left. She turns the left skate to point left.

2. She bends the right knee slightly and inserts right knee into the back of the left knee. Five-Hole should be closed and body facing puck as goalie crosses the net to the left.

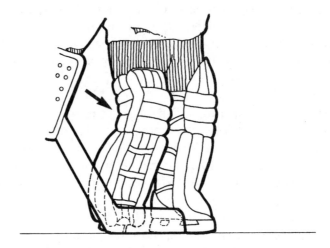

3. She pushes off with right skate towards the left.

Fundamental #3

MOTION: THE ADVANCED ELEMENT

THEORY

If goalies only faced stationary shooters, it would be enough to "cover the angles." However, the puck is always moving and the goalie has to move as well in order to maintain good angles and face the shooter. There are five basic kinds of motion a goalie must master:
- forward;
- backward;
- lateral move to the left;
- lateral move to the right;
- up and down.

DESCRIPTION

Forward Movement

A goalie must move forward to "challenge" shooters. By skating directly towards a shooter, the goaltender reduces the amount of net available to that shooter.

Backward Movement

Once the shooter gets closer to the goalie (that is, once the shooter reaches the face-off circle hash marks) the goalie has to move backward to avoid being caught too far out from the net.

Lateral Right and Left Movement

A skilled forward line will keep the play moving from side to side, trying to pull the goalie and defence out of position. Also, a forward bearing down on a goalie will try to move the play from side to side. A goaltender must be able to follow such lateral play. When the play is well out from the net, the goalie uses the shuffle; for close-in play, the T-Push.

Up/Down Movement

We've all heard the colour commentators complain about a goalie who drops down to the ice. In fact, the problem is not with goalies who go down, but with goalies who don't get back up. Goalies go down to block low shots, deflections, screen shots and lateral plays. With beginners, the coach should worry about one thing: that a goalie who goes down can get back up again.

COACHING TIPS

While the concept of motion is not difficult to understand — the goalie is basically following the play — it is difficult to execute. Rather than provide a check sheet for motion, we recommend a simple exercise called The Five-Point Drill (or "Hit The Deck!" for younger goalies). Goalies at any level, even the pros, should do this drill at least once a practice.

THE FIVE-POINT DRILL

Goalies face the coach. The coach calls out a series of directions: "Forward; backward; shuffle left; shuffle right; T-Push left; T-Push right; down; up." The goalies follow the directions the coach gives them. The coach increases the intensity of the drill as it progresses.

We recommend no more than 30 seconds of this drill at a time for young goalies, although you can alternate drill and rest — 30 second drill, rest, drill, rest — for several minutes. This drill is very tiring, so you might want to save it until the end of practice. Also, to make it more fun for younger goalies, treat this drill as a game. Instead of saying "down," say "Hit the Deck." A simple change like this turns a cumbersome drill into an enjoyable interlude for some kids.

A checklist for the Five-Point Drill follows. This allows coaches to use the drill for both evaluation and skill development. Pay attention to lateral movement — most of us favour our strong side and need to work on our weak side. Also, watch that goalies maintain stance throughout the drill. Remember, the Five-Point Drill should be used at every practice.

CHECKLIST
Five-Point Drill

☐ **Forward Motion — Was the goalie's forward motion smooth, with minimal foot, leg, backside or shoulder movement? Did the goalie maintain stance, keep the stick on the ice and face the shooter (i.e. the coach)?**

☐ **Backward Motion — Was the goalie's backward motion smooth, with minimal foot, leg, backside or shoulder movement? Did the goalie maintain stance, keep the gloves up, keep the stick on the ice and face the shooter? Did the goalie keep the Five-Hole consistent?**

☐ **Stops and Starts — Were the goalie's transitions sharp, with quick stops and starts in a new direction? Did the goalie maintain stance, keep the stick on the ice and face the shooter?**

☐ **Lateral Motion: Shuffle — Could the goalie shuffle to the left and the right? Did the goalie maintain stance, keep the stick on the ice and face the shooter while shuffling both left and right?**

☐ **Lateral Motion: T-Push — Did the goalie use the T-Push both left and right? Did the goalie allow only a minimal gap in the Five-Hole, keep the stick on the ice and face the shooter while T-Pushing both left and right?**

☐ **Up and Down Motion — After going down, did the goalie quickly get back up and quickly resume the stance?**

SECTION 2:

POSITIONAL PLAY IN MOTION

So far, we have given you the basics of positional play, trying to keep things in their simplest terms. But what does a goaltender do in the course of a game, when things are not so simple? In practical terms, how does a goaltender set positional play into motion?

At the start, we said that the goaltender's basic function is to defend the net. Let's refine this statement: the goaltender's primary aim is to establish and maintain optimum defensive position. When the play is in motion, this is a three-step process:

1. The goalie establishes position in the net.
2. The goalie approximates optimum position.
3. The goalie moves directly towards that position.

This three-step process is repeated over and over throughout the course of the game. Most goalies are never aware that they use this strategy. Let's look at this strategy one step at a time, and in the process we will deal with two new elements: the *Goalie-Net Relationship* and *Telescoping*.

KEY CONCEPT
The three steps to establishing optimum defensive position are:

1. Goalie establishes position in relation to the net (the Goalie-Net Relationship).
2. Goalie selects optimum position (Telescoping).
3. Goalie moves to optimum position.

Fundamental #4

THE GOALIE-NET RELATIONSHIP: ESTABLISHING POSITION

THEORY

Goalies need to know where they are standing in relation to their net at all times. However, they rarely have the time to look behind to see where the net is. They need a system to help.

DESCRIPTION

There are two main ways goalies can establish position without turning their heads: 1) tapping the short-side post, and 2) using the face-off circle hash marks as reference points.

Tapping the short-side post:

The "short side" refers to the side of the goalie closest to the nearest post. If the goalie is in the left half of the crease, the left side is the short side. To "see" where the post is without looking, goalies tap the nearest post with their stick. This is done with the least possible disruption of stance.

Using the hash marks for reference:

While tapping the post helps set the goalie's bearings when the play is in close, the goalie can use the hash marks on the edge of the face-off circles when the play is further out. The goalie approximates the central point between these marks. Standing in line with this point puts the goalie in the centre of the net.

COACHING TIPS

Awareness of position in the net must become second nature. It's the kind of skill that goalies only develop through constant practice. We recommend the Three-Point Drill. Have your goalies go through this drill at least once at every practice.

THE THREE-POINT DRILL

The goalie stands in the crease facing open ice. The coach stands behind the net to check on the goalie's positioning. The coach calls out: "Left Post, Right Post, and Centre."

"Left" and "Right" mean that the goalie is to move quickly to that side of the net; "Post" means the goalie is to tap the near-side post with the stick; "Centre" means the goalie should move to the top and middle of the crease. This is a very simple drill. Spend only a few minutes on it at every practice.

Variation

Coach calls out "Shuffle left/right" or "Push left/right" (push = T-Push) so that the goalie can work on specific skating techniques.

The coach is watching for:

- A smooth T-Push or shuffle across the front of the net.
- A goalie who taps the post without looking, and without major disruption to stance.
- A goalie who moves to the centre of the crease without disrupting stance.

Fundamental #5

TELESCOPING: APPROXIMATING OPTIMUM POSITION

THEORY

Once goalies know their position in the net, they need to decide where the line of angle is and how far out they should go to block an angle. Telescoping allows goalies to visualize this optimum distance.

DESCRIPTION

Look at some object on the wall like a clock or small picture. Extend your finger towards it and close one eye. Now, move your finger towards your eye. At some point, your finger will totally block your view of the object on the wall. The same principle is behind telescoping: you are trying to find that point where your body totally blocks the shooter's view of the net.

To understand telescoping, it helps to draw a diagram:

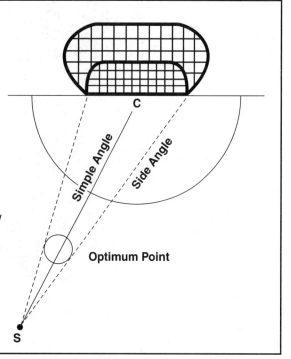

TELESCOPING

Draw an overhead view of a net and select a point in front of that net where the shot is coming from.

Draw a line from the centre of the goal line to the point-of-shot. This is your simple angle.

Draw lines from the left and right posts to the point-of-shot. These are your side guidelines.

Put your little finger on the paper and see how far up the simplest angle line you have to move it until the side guidelines are covered as well. This is your optimum point: the point where with the least amount of distance moved covers the net.

COACHING TIPS

Like "simple angles," "telescoping" is an abstract geometric notion and it might take time for some kids to pick it up. Don't worry! Many pros have gone through their careers without knowing that "telescoping" exists. As with any abstract idea, it's always helpful to use as many concrete examples as possible. This is a case where pictures do tell a thousand words.

Fundamental #6

TAKING POSITION: MOVING DIRECTLY TO THE OPTIMUM POSITION

After all the hard work we've done in this section, it's nice to finish off with something easy. Once goalies establish their position in relation to the net and decide on the optimum position, they simply skate directly towards it. There's not a lot we can say here. It's important to remember, however, that everything we've learned about positional play — Stance, Angles, Motion, Telescoping and the Goalie-Net Relationship — has built up to this final, simple motion.

Grant Fuhr takes his stance.

2. PUCK PLAY

REACTING TO A SHOT AND RESPONDING TO THE CONSEQUENCES

INTRODUCTION: THE DYNAMICS OF A SAVE

The Big Save. That's what most people think goaltending is all about. It's the mythic element of the game: the lone goalie rides into town to save the day.

In fact, making a save is much less mysterious than all that. The coach who understands the dynamics of a save can help goalies improve their save percentage.

Each save is really a three-step process. First, a goalie establishes and maintains optimum position (which includes proper stance). Second, the goalie forms a plan: "Will I stop play or keep it going?" Both these steps are conscious actions. The third step happens very quickly: the goalie reacts to the shot. This is an automatic response, a reaction. There is only one way goalies become adept at such reactions: effective practice.

We covered the first step in the last chapter. In this chapter we will look at how goalies develop a plan and then at how they can build their "save" skills. Our focus last chapter was on evaluation. In this chapter, the focus is on practice. We describe on-ice sessions you can incorporate into your practice routine.

These sessions are broken into two parts: In Section 1 we look at how goalies use different pieces of equipment (that is, different parts of the body) to make a save; Section 2 covers the different shot situations goalies face. These sessions are progressive. They not only build a goaltender's save skills and reaction time, they also enhance the shooting skills of your other players.

THE PLAN

As in any successful venture, goalies begin the save process with a plan. Goalies must ask themselves: "What am I going to do with the puck once I make the save? Will I stop play, or keep it going?"

The goalie's decision is a team decision. The rule is: if the team is under pressure, the goalie stops play; if the team is not under pressure, the goalie keeps the play going. The goalie either directs the puck out of danger or passes it to a teammate.

What do we mean by pressure? Any of these situations could apply:

- Opposition players are near the net.
- The goalie is tired, or a teammate is tired from a long shift.
- The goalie or another player has lost a stick.
- The opposition team has taken several shots in a short period of time, and the goalie wants to halt their momentum.

At more advanced levels, the goalie's plans are more sophisticated and take into account things like face-off percentages and the puck-clearing ability of a defenceman. At this beginner level, coaches just need to pass on one message to their goalies: "Have a plan."

PUTTING THE PLAN INTO PRACTICE

The sessions that follow help you to build planning into each practice exercise. You will find that each exercise works with both the "stop play" and "continue play" options.

Goalies who want to stop play have three choices:
1. Catch the puck and hold onto it.
2. Cover up the puck on the ice ("freeze" the puck).
3. Deflect the puck over the glass and out of play.

Goalies who want to continue play have three choices:
1. Deflect the puck (with leg pads, blocker, skate or stick) out of danger, preferably to the corner of the rink.
2. Gain control of the puck and pass it to a teammate.
3. Deflect the puck out of danger (with leg pads, blocker, skate or stick) to a teammate.

PUCKHANDLING

The complete goalie needs top-notch puckhandling skills. Unfortunately, goalies are often left out of passing and shooting drills, or are allowed to use their cumbersome gloves as an excuse to slack off during those drills. While it is true that the gloves do take some getting used to, make sure your goalies participate in puckhandling drills and expect the same level of commitment from them that you expect from every other player.

While many pro goalies shoot the opposite way they catch (e.g. a right-handed catcher will shoot left-handed) and use a curved stick, we recommend that beginner goalies shoot in their normal way and use a straight stick. We are not rigid traditionalists. We just think that the developing goalie should concentrate on the fundamentals. Fancy stickwork comes later.

SECTION 1:

USING THE EQUIPMENT

In this section we look at how goalies use their equipment and bodies to make a save. We break this process into four elements:

1. *Optimum Position*: Adapting what we learned in Concept #1 (stance, angles, motion) to specific situations, to increase the save potential.
2. *Concentration*: Goalies must follow the puck at all times, from the moment it leaves the shooter's stick to the moment it strikes the goalie's equipment (we call this the "point of contact").
3. *Control*: Goalies should use their equipment to absorb a shot. This gives goalies more control over a rebound.
4. *Plan:* Goalies should always have a plan in mind *before* they make a save.

In the following seven sessions we discuss these elements as they apply to different kinds of saves. As well, at the end of each session we include a Training Exercise, designed to build both a goalie's plan/save skills and shooters' accuracy. There is also a Speed Variation, a more advanced exercise designed to improve your goalie's reflexes. For experienced players, we've included a Comprehensive Shot/Save Exercise at the end of Section 1.

Remember, the point in all these exercises is to build skill, not demonstrate it. It's important that you allow your novice goalies time to set up properly between shooters. The development of your goalies will be substantially enhanced if they learn these techniques the right way from the start.

Curtis Joseph concentrates on the game.

Save Session #1:

USING THE TRAPPER

OPTIMUM POSITION

The glovehand side is usually a goalie's strong-point. Remember, the trapper should be kept at knee height, just above the leg pad. The trapper should be open at all times (except, of course, when the puck is inside of it). The goalie should squeeze the trapper shut once the puck is inside it.

CONCENTRATION

Watch the puck from the moment it leaves a shooter's stick until it reaches the goalie's glove.

CONTROL

The goalie's catching arm should be relaxed. This allows the arm to "give" a little more when the puck reaches it, making the shot easier to hold and control.

PLAN

A rebound off the trapper leaves the goalie very vulnerable. In practice, have beginner goalies catch and hold the puck. (Later, they may choose to drop it to continue play if their team is under no pressure.)

TRAINING EXERCISE

(10 minutes maximum)

Have your shooters line up in front of the goalie, close enough so that their shots will reach the net, but not so close that the goalie has no time to react. Have them shoot puck after puck at the goalie's trapper side. Start off with slow shots and allow lots of time between shots. You are using this exercise to work on two things: the goalie's save technique, as outlined above, and the shooter's accuracy. Remember, with trapper-side shots, the goalie's plan is to always catch the puck. You may repeat this exercise for a couple of practices, until you feel your goalie has a good sense of the proper trapper technique.

Speed Variation

To build quickness in a goalie with good technique, have the goalie stand off-centre, leaving lots of net exposed on the trapper side. Allow the shooters to increase speed until their shots are faster than the goalie's reaction time and most of the shots are going in. You will find that when goalies are forced to move quickly, their quickness improves. Remember to explain what you're doing to your goalies so that this doesn't simply become an exercise in frustration.

Save Session #2:

USING THE BLOCKER

OPTIMUM POSITION

The glove should be at knee level, just above the leg pads. Make sure that the glove in the back of the blocker does not restrict your goalie's fingers and grip. Often, this glove is sewn right into the blocker, which doesn't allow the goalie to grip the stick properly. Also, some goalies like to bend their blockers, giving them a banana shape. This does help cushion shots, but a bent blocker covers much less area and reduces the goalie's control over rebounds. We prefer a flat blocker.

CONCENTRATION

Watch the puck from the moment it leaves the shooter's stick until it strikes the blocker.

CONTROL

Move the blocker backwards slightly as the puck approaches. This cushions the shot, reducing the chance of a rebound.

PLAN

When goalies want to stop the play, they can either pin the puck on their blocker with their trapper or drop to the ice to cover the rebound. When goalies want to continue the play, they angle the blocker in the direction they want the puck to go. With pressure in front of the net, the goalie may choose to deflect the puck to the corner or out of play rather than risk giving up a stick-side rebound.

TRAINING EXERCISE

(5 to 7 minutes maximum)

Line up shooters as before. Remember: the shooters are practicing accuracy, not goal scoring. Break the exercise into two parts. In the first part, tell goalies to stop the play. It's important to allow them time between shots to cover the rebounds. In the second part, tell goalies to continue play: they should deflect pucks to the corner or behind the net.

Speed Variation

With more experienced goalies who demonstrate good blocker technique, try this variation. Have the goalie stand off-centre, leaving lots of open net on the blocker side. Have shooters increase the speed of their shots.

Save Session #3:

USING THE CHEST AND STOMACH

OPTIMUM POSITION

On medium-high shots ("belly shots"), a goalie should avoid standing up as the puck comes into the chest — the bent body creates a pocket with the chest protector that cushions the shot. This tends to direct rebounds closer to the goalie. On higher shots ("chest shots"), the goalie must "jump" or extend the body upwards to make the save. If a shot is obviously over the net, it should be left alone.

Make sure the chest protector is loose fitting: this allows flexibility and provides proper protection. Also, we encourage goalies at all levels to use throat protectors.

CONCENTRATION

Goalies should follow the puck from the moment it leaves the shooter's stick until it is close to contact with the chest protector. Often, when the puck gets close to the chest the mask will momentarily obscure sight of the puck. Also, goalies may lose sight of the puck in their equipment.

CONTROL

Proper stance creates a big pocket around the stomach which helps absorb the shot. In this case, as in most others, it helps to skate backwards slowly and smoothly.

PLAN

Because a shot to the belly or chest creates control problems for goalies — they will often lose sight of the puck — they should strive to control the puck. This means pinning it to the chest protector with one or both gloves, or quickly covering the rebound near the feet.

TRAINING EXERCISE

(5 to 7 minutes)
Line up shooters as before. Now they are shooting at the chest (if your shooters are accurate, there should be no goals scored). Watch that the goalie remains crouched for the "belly shots" and extends for "shoulder shots." Leave enough time between shots for the goalie to gain control of the puck, then regain proper position.

Speed Variation

With more experienced goalies, increase the speed of the shots and reduce the time between shots. Do not use this variation with goalies who do not have a throat protector.

Save Session #4:

USING THE STICK

OPTIMUM POSITION

The goalie's stick blade is flat on the ice, slightly ahead of the skate toes. Make sure your goalies have the proper lie on their sticks (the lie is the angle between the shaft of the stick and the blade). If a goalie has a lot of trouble with ice shots, there is a good chance that he or she has the wrong lie on the stick.

It's easy to check for the proper lie. If the stick blade does not sit flat on the ice when a goalie goes into the stance, the lie is not right.

CONCENTRATION

Goalies should follow the puck from the moment it leaves the shooter's stick until it makes contact with their own stick.

CONTROL

Goalies must not hold the stick too tightly. They should allow the momentum of the shot to push the stick back into the skate toes or, in the case of a butterfly save, against the leg pads. As usual, goalies should skate backwards slowly and smoothly.

PLAN

When goalies want to stop play, they will have to drop to the ice to cover the puck, either with their leg pads or trapper. When they want play to continue, they direct the shot to the nearest corner (for example, a shot to the right side of the net gets directed to the right corner).

TRAINING EXERCISE

(5 to 7 minutes)
Line up shooters as before. Have them aim for the blade of the goalie's stick; wrist shots will work best. Split the exercise into two parts, with the goalie both stopping and continuing the play.

Speed Variation

With more experienced goalies, increase the speed of shots and decrease time between shots.

Save Session #5:

USING THE SKATES

OPTIMUM POSITION

Goalies usually make skate saves on shots to a low corner. The goalie uses the T-Push to make the skate save. The goalie turns the save skate in the direction the rebound should go, bends the other leg slightly and pushes towards the puck with this leg. The bent knee should drop to the ice to maximize lateral distance of the "save" skate, and for goalie comfort. Once the skate save is made, the goalie must quickly resume proper stance.

CONCENTRATION

Goalies should follow the puck from the moment it leaves the shooter's stick until it hits their own skates (if possible). A lot of times, when the shot is coming from the side of the rink — and especially if the shooter is on the goalie's off-wing — the goalie will line up the angle with the player rather than with the puck. The goalie must concentrate on the puck to stay in position. After the save is made, the goalie must get back up as quickly as possible. This is a very important point: whenever goalies go down, they must get back up right away. Let them know if they forget!

CONTROL

In this situation, a goalie does not want to absorb the shot. The goalie should deliberately push the skate towards the puck, to redirect the puck as far away from the net as possible. Then the goalie must move quickly to gain control of the rebound.

PLAN

Skate saves leave goalies very vulnerable — they wind up out of position and out of the proper stance. The plan is always the same: to direct the puck to the nearest corner with as much force as possible.

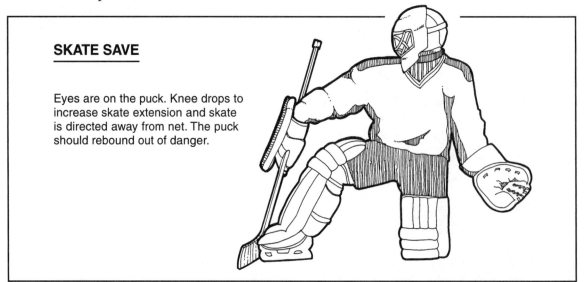

SKATE SAVE

Eyes are on the puck. Knee drops to increase skate extension and skate is directed away from net. The puck should rebound out of danger.

TRAINING EXERCISE
(5 to 7 minutes)
Have shooters line up as usual, then run through the four variations in this exercise.

1. Shooters aim low to the right post. This is a difficult shot for a lot of players to make so it is good practice (once again, wrist shots work best). The goalie tries to direct all shots to the nearest corner.
2. Shooters aim low to the left post. Goalie: same as above. Remember that the goalie must move quickly to cover shots that do not clear the goal area. Also remember that the goalie mush resume the proper stance right away.
3. Repeat Variation 1, but this time goalie is without a stick.
4. Repeat Variation 2, but this time goalie is without a stick.

Speed Variation
With more experienced goalies, repeat the four variations with faster shots and less time between shots.

Save Session #6:

USING THE LEG PADS

OPTIMUM POSITION

In the proper stance, goalies' knees are bent slightly and the legs are open below the knees to form an inverted V. Goalies start high in the crease, even a little beyond it if possible, which allows them to shift backward as shots come in. This motion cushions the shots and helps draw the puck into the pads.

With medium high shots (knee high), goalies do not want to go down until after the initial save is made — and then, only to cover the rebound. Bent knees are vital to this kind of save: a straight, rigid leg results in a fast rebound in front of the net.

With low shots, goalies go down — they drop into the "butterfly" position. That is, they drop down to their knees and push their skates and leg pads to the sides, to cover the lower corners. When in the butterfly position, goalies have their sticks in front of the Five-Hole and keep their knees tightly together. If goalies do not stop play, they must get back onto their feet right away.

CONCENTRATION

Goalies should follow the puck from the moment it leaves the shooter's stick until it makes contact with the pads.

CONTROL

Legs should be relaxed; rigid legs will lead to big rebounds. As mentioned already, the goalie should establish a smooth backward motion.

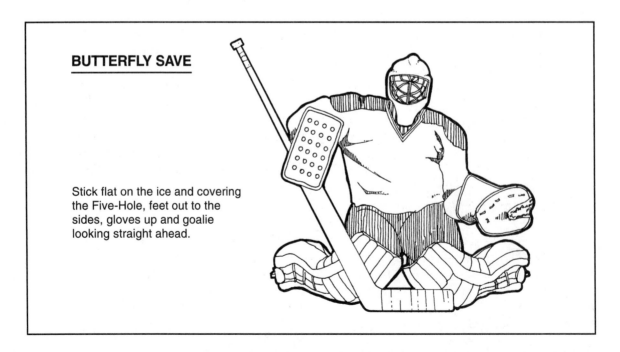

BUTTERFLY SAVE

Stick flat on the ice and covering the Five-Hole, feet out to the sides, gloves up and goalie looking straight ahead.

PLAN

When goalies want to stop play, they draw the puck into their body, as described above. When goalies go down for a leg save, they will want to stop play — they are on the ice and therefore out of position. Remember that they must return to their feet right away if play is not stopped.

TRAINING EXERCISE

(5 to 7 minutes)

Line up shooters as usual. They are to shoot knee-high and lower. First, have them shoot to the right side of the net; then to the centre; and, finally, to the left side. Goalies must try to stop the play. Do not let your goalies get away with lazy or half-finished responses — either they cover the puck completely or they direct it to the nearest corner and, if necessary, return to their feet right away. Remember, your goalies start high and maintain a backward motion.

Speed Variation

With more experienced goalies, increase shot speed and decrease set-up time between shots. As always, remind goalies that in speed drills you are not looking for saves but for increased quickness.

A NOTE ON THE FIVE-HOLE

The Five-Hole is the space between the goalie's leg pads, from the knees down to the ice. For some reason, many people think that goalies should never allow a goal to be scored through the Five-Hole. Nothing could be further from the truth.

The Five-Hole is the most vulnerable spot on a goalie. In this manual, we favour a style of play that leaves the Five-Hole somewhat exposed. The Inverted-V Style has goalies playing with their legs apart. This allows greater protection of the bottom low corners, with less protection of the Five-Hole. Look at it this way: with the Inverted-V Style, two vulnerable spots are protected, leaving one spot open. In the traditional Stand-Up Style, the Five-Hole is covered, but the two corners are left open. With the Inverted-V Style, it's also easier for goalies to go down to their knees (to protect the Five-Hole) and to get back up on their feet.

The best advice we can give goalies is to become strong skaters, to work very hard on lateral movement, and to practice going down to the knees and getting back up again. Do not worry about the occasional shot that sneaks through the Five-Hole. It's just part of today's game.

Save Session #7:

STACKING THE LEG PADS

OPTIMUM POSITION
Goalies should only "stack the pads" when the play is close to the net and they have to cover a quick pass across the net. Instruct the goalie to assume proper stance. When the pass comes, the goalie should lunge feet-first towards the pass receiver. The goalie wants to wind up on the ice lying sideways, with one pad directly on top of the other. The free arm is straight at the goalie's side, slightly away from the body. The object is to cover as much space as possible.

CONCENTRATION
Goalies must watch the puck from the time it leaves the passer's stick to the moment it contacts the shooter's stick to the point of goalie contact.

CONTROL
It is difficult to absorb shots in these situations because the goalie will be moving towards the shooter.

PLAN
This is a desperate situation. The goalie's main concern is the initial shot. Goalies should stop play, if possible; in most situations, however, they must be prepared to return to their feet right away.

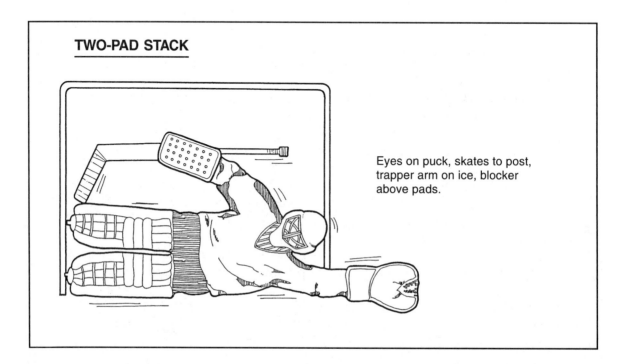

TWO-PAD STACK

Eyes on puck, skates to post, trapper arm on ice, blocker above pads.

TRAINING EXERCISE
(6 to 8 minutes)
Have shooters form two groups. One group lines up to the goalie's right, a foot above the crease. The other group lines up to the goalie's left, ten feet to the side of the net and a foot above the crease. One at a time, a player from the first group passes to a player in the second group. The goalie covers the shot, lunging across the net into the two-pad position. Have the players switch roles and, once everyone has had a turn shooting, switch sides (that is, have the pass come from the left side). Give the goalie time to re-establish position before each pass.

Note: a lot of goals will be scored during this exercise, so remind the goalie that the point is to practice the two-pad stack. When they do happen, saves during this exercise are both spectacular and deeply satisfying.

Speed Variation
With a more experienced goalie, run the exercise as above but have the players in motion, skating down on the goalie.

COMPREHENSIVE SHOT/SAVE DRILL

Combining all the Training Exercises in Section 1 creates a Comprehensive Shot/Save Drill for all players. With younger players, work through the first seven sessions in this chapter, then use this drill at practices thereafter. With older players, you may start this drill at the first practice.

Have all your shooters line up just outside the hash marks (with younger shooters, move in as close as necessary). Tell your players what part of the net they are to shoot at ("top right"; "bottom right"; "Five-Hole"; "chest area" etc.), and allow them to take turns shooting. It's important that the coach keep the shooters on target. Have each player take two or three shots at each target area before moving on, and make sure you spend time on each of the six target areas. When done properly, this is a very tiring drill for a goalie. Give the goalie a rest every five minutes (there is a natural break every time the players go to collect their pucks), or if you have more than one goalie, alternate.

Speed Variations
- Move the shooters close in once the goalie is warmed up.
- Reduce the wait between shots until it becomes a rapid-fire drill.
- Have the shooters alternate from the left side to the right side so that the goalie practices moving across the net.
- Have players start at the red line, and shoot from either the blueline or the face-off circle; alternate left and right sides.
- Practice "stop play" and "continue play."

WHAT THE COACH IS LOOKING FOR
- That shooters are on target.
- That the goalie establishes optimum position, or re-establishes position after making a save.
- Goalies' weak areas. If a goalies has trouble in one area, spend extra time working it.

Note: when you are pushing your goalies, they can become very frustrated. The odd temper tantrum or angry outburst can be expected.

COACHING TIPS
This is a drill for both goaltenders and shooters. It is very important that the players shoot at the target areas and that you spend a lot of time on each target area. Some will argue that this does not mimic a game situation: the goalie knows where the puck is going. True, but this is not a game situation; this is a practice drill. The way to improve technique and reaction time is to repeat a drill over and over again. In a game, goalies and shooters rarely have time to think about shots; the coach's job is to help players practice conscious *actions* until they become automatic *reactions*.

You can also use this drill as your pre-game warm-up. Too many coaches allow their players to have disorganized and dangerous warm-ups — the goalie is just a moving target at which the other players blast a puck. In fact, the point of the pre-game warm-up is to help get the goalie ready for a game. So why not do it in a safe and systematic way?

SECTION 2:

SHOT SITUATIONS

Now that you understand how goaltenders use their equipment and bodies to make a save, let's look at the kinds of shot situations goalies face during a game. We've broken these sessions into three elements:

1. *Definition*: defines the particular shot situation.
2. *Optimum Position*: stance, angles and motion, along with points covered in the last section — all as they apply to specific shot situations.
3. *Plan*: as before, the goalie must know where the play is heading before the shot is taken.

We have included a training exercise in each session. Unlike the exercises in the first section, which combine to form the Comprehensive Save/Shot Drill, these exercises are meant to be used on their own. This is because they are time-consuming and no coach is going to spend most of every practice working on a goalie's save skills (although it would be great if you did!). Go through one session per practice. After that, you might want to rotate through these sessions again, or you might want to work on specific shot situations as the need arises. For example, if on Tuesday's game your goalie lets in six ice shots, you might want to review the Ice Shot Session at Thursday's practice.

Rick Tabarrachi anticipates a shot.

Shot Situation #1:

POINT, MID-ICE AND LONG SHOTS

DEFINITIONS

A "point shot" is a shot from the blueline. A "mid-ice shot" is a shot from the space between the blueline up to the top of the face-off circle. A "long shot" is a shot from beyond the blueline.

OPTIMUM POSITION

The goalie should come out as far as possible — at least three feet beyond the crease — to cut down the angle. As the shot is taken, or as the shooter moves towards the net, the goalie should glide backwards smoothly. This motion:

• gives the goalie some backward momentum in case the play moves in close to the net or across the ice;

• helps the goalie absorb the shot to control the rebound.

If the play moves from side-to-side on mid-ice and long shots, the goalie uses the shuffle step to maintain position. On a long shot, the goalie must move well out, maintain stance and concentrate. It is difficult to focus on the puck coming in from that distance.

PLAN

A goalie who is in proper position should rarely have to go down on shots from this far out. The exception might be on shots to the low corners (but if the goalie is out far enough, this should not be a problem). The goalie's plan in this situation is to either direct the puck to the corner, or to gain control of the puck and play it to a teammate.

TRAINING EXERCISE

(5 to 7 minutes)

Have your shooters line up on the blueline. They may shoot from anywhere between the blueline and the top of the face-off circle (pylons may be used to help define the boundaries). Have them shoot in turn on your cue (for example, one short blow on your whistle). In this exercise, the shooters try to score. Give the goalie time to re-establish position between shots.

Next, form two lines at the blue line, one on the left side of the rink and one on the right. Have one player from each line step forward. Instruct the two players to play as a unit. They are allowed one or two passes across the rink, then a shot. Boundaries are as before.

Finally, have the players shoot from beyond the blueline. Although the long shot is seldom seen in a game, it often results in a goal. The reason? The curved stick causes the puck to dip and flutter and, over a long distance, the changes can be sudden and dramatic. Take a little time working on this shot so that your goalie learns to expect the unexpected.

Speed Variation

As goalies become more comfortable and faster, have players shoot on the move and reduce the time between shots. Also, have players come down in pairs, with one shooting off the other's pass.

LONG SHOTS

Goalie comes out at least three feet, always maintaining proper stance and using the telescope technique.

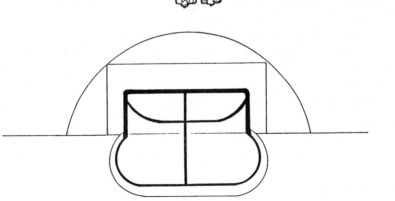

CHECKLIST
For Point, Mid-Ice and Long Shots

☐ Goalie comes out far enough to cover the angle.

☐ Goalie comes well out — at least three feet — to play the long shot.

☐ Goalie starts to move back as the shot is taken or as the shooter moves forward.

☐ Goalie does not go down, except to cover the low corners or smother a rebound.

☐ Goalie completes the play — that is, the goalie directs the shot to the corner or controls the puck (covers and holds it).

☐ Goalie maintains proper stance and always faces the shooter.

☐ Goalie follows the shot from the shooter's stick to the point of contact.

☐ Goalie plays the puck, not the shooter.

☐ Goalie uses the shuffle to maintain position when the puck moves from side to side, with the play out of the net.

☐ Goalie re-establishes position as quickly as possible after making a save.

Shot Situation #2:

SLOT SHOTS

DEFINITION

The "slot" is the area in front of the net, from the face-off circle hash marks down to the crease. It extends a couple of feet to the right and left of the posts. Mark off the boundaries of the slot with pylons. A slot shot is most often a pass to the player in the slot area; the player shoots the puck right away without stopping it or trying to gain control of it. This is how we will practice the slot shot.

OPTIMUM POSITION

Goalies should move from the side of the net to cover the centre of the net. They need to remain on their feet and quickly move to the top of the crease or higher.

PLAN

The goalie wants to take as much of the net away from the shooter as possible. Because the likelihood of a rebound is high and the goalie will not have much time to react, the goalie must be ready to re-establish optimum position immediately after the save. Ideally, the goalie will direct the puck away from the net or stop play right away.

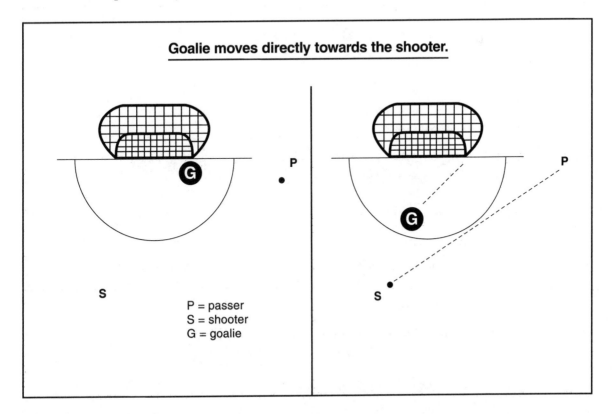

Goalie moves directly towards the shooter.

P = passer
S = shooter
G = goalie

TRAINING EXERCISE
(5 to 7 minutes)

Mark off slot boundaries with pylons. Form two lines: one in the slot (the shooters) and one to the side of the slot (the passers). The players switch lines once they have taken their turns. Each player shoots the puck in the following four situations:

1. High in slot, with pass coming from the right side.
2. High in slot, with pass coming from the left side.
3. Middle of slot, with pass coming from the right side.
4. Middle of slot, with pass coming from the left side.

Players must shoot the puck directly off the pass; they are not to stop the pass and try to take control of the puck. If a player starts to play the puck, blow your whistle to stop the play. If a pass is off the mark, give the passer another chance.

Each time, the goalie starts out tight against the near post (the post closest to the pass). Give the goalie time to re-establish this position after each shot.

Speed Variation

Reduce set-up time between shots.

CHECKLIST
For Slot Shots

☐ Goalie should stay on feet and drive towards the shot, anticipating a quick rebound.

☐ Goalie should complete the play: either stop play (first choice) or redirect the puck out of danger.

☐ Goalie maintains proper stance, when appropriate, and always faces the shooter.

☐ Goalie follows the shot from the passer's stick to the shooter's stick, to the point of contact. Concentration is essential.

☐ After going down, goalie either covers up the puck or returns to feet right away.

☐ Goalie plays the puck, not the shooter.

Shot Situation #3:

BREAKAWAY, TWO-ON-ZERO, PENALTY SHOT

DEFINITION

A "breakaway" is when the shooter is coming in all alone on the goalie, with the defence out of the play. From a goalie's perspective, there are two different kinds of breakaways: straight on (with the shooter coming up the centre of the ice), and from the side (with the player coming down the wing). Each type is played differently. The penalty shot, which always starts at the centre-ice dot, is played as a breakaway.

We will also look at the two-on-zero play: two forwards coming in on the goalie with no defencemen in the play.

OPTIMUM POSITION
General

In all three situations, the goalie starts high out of the net — ten feet beyond the crease. The goalie moves backward, slowly and smoothly, as the player approaches, taking care to maintain stance (the goalie must not drop shoulders or gloves, nor widen space between the legs).

The goalie should not back too far into the net — many shooters simply wait for the goalie to back into the net then shoot into an open corner. The goalie should slow down once he or she reaches the crease, but should not stop. The goalie wants to stay moving and on his or her feet for as long as possible. If players get in close, the goalie should use the T-Push to follow the play across the crease.

Shooters coming up the centre of the ice

The goalie should start well out of the net — as far out as the face-off circle hash marks. The goalie should move backwards slowly as shooters approach. If the goalie covers the angles properly, shooters either waste a shot, by shooting into the goalie, or they try to deke. In a deke, shooters try to fake the goalie into going down early or into moving out of position. The goalie must stay up for as long as possible and follow the play in close using the T-Push. At all times, the goalie must watch the puck, not the player.

Shooter coming down the wing

The goalie starts high again, moving straight out from the near post to the angle point (see "Telescoping"). The goalie moves backward, slowly and smoothly, as the shooter approaches. Again, the goalie should stay on his or her feet as long as possible, and use the T-Push to follow the play across the crease.

Two-on-zero

The strategy here is similar to the one used in the breakaway. The goalie starts high and progresses backwards slowly and smoothly. The backward motion allows the goalie to react to a pass, should it come. The goalie should not get caught too far out of the net or, in particular, too far to one side of the net. This will allow for a pass and an easy goal.

The goalie plays the puck, but is aware that a pass may be made at any time. If the pass is made out from the crease, the goalie uses the shuffle skate to re-establish position. If the pass comes in close to the net, the goalie uses the T-Push or two-pad stack. As in the slot shot, the goalie wants to drive towards the shot when it comes off a pass in close. This will reduce the amount of net available to shooters.

Although the goalie wants to move backwards as a shot or player approaches, he or she does not want to get caught too far back in the crease. Often, young goalies will move to the back of the crease automatically; perhaps it feels safer. Don't let them develop this costly habit.

PLAN

Goalies are under pressure; they want to stop play if possible. Rebounds are always a problem — goalies want to direct the puck as far away from the net as possible. That said, their main concern is the initial shot; this is where their energy should be focused.

TRAINING EXERCISE
(10 minutes)
Shooters and goalies both enjoy this exercise. Have shooters line up beyond the blueline. In turn, they move in alone on the goalie. Have each shooter take a turn:

1. Going straight down the ice.
2. Going down the right side of the rink.
3. Going down the left side of the rink.

Afterwards, split shooters into two lines and have them try the two-on-zero play. Have the goalie start at the top of the crease as each shooter begins; allow the goalie time between each shooter to re-establish this position. Allow shooters no more than three passes. Remember to keep breakaway scenarios realistic: shooters should maintain forward motion and make plays quickly, as if there were defencemen in chase.

Speed Variation
Reduce the set-up time between shooters.

CHECKLIST
For Breakaway, Two-on-Zero and Penalty Shots

☐ Goalie starts high — near the hash marks when the player comes up the centre, and a comparable distance from the net when the player comes in on the wing.

☐ Goalie establishes and maintains a slow, smooth backward motion.

☐ Goalie maintains stance: does not drop shoulders or glove; doesn't open Five-Hole beyond normal stance.

☐ Goalie does not move too far back into the net.

☐ Goalie stays on feet for as long as possible.

☐ Goalie uses T-Push to follow the play beyond the crease. After going down, goalie either covers up the puck or returns to feet right away.

☐ Goalie does not move too far to one side on a two-on-zero.

☐ Goalie plays the puck at all times, not the shooter.

Shot Situation #4:

SCREEN SHOTS

DEFINITION

A "screen" shot is a shot that's taken when other players are standing in front of the net, restricting the goalie's view.

OPTIMUM POSITION

Screen shots require a quick reaction from goalies. Goalies want to strike a balance between position and visibility: they want to cover as much of the net as possible without losing sight of the puck.

The first step is for the goalie to locate the puck. Next, the goalie moves towards the puck, to cover the angle. The goalie does not want to come out too far beyond the crease unless the shooter seems committed to the shot. Otherwise, the goalie is vulnerable to a pass. The goalie also doesn't want to get mixed up in traffic in front of the goal. Traffic restricts the goalie's visibility and ability to move across the net to cover the play.

The goalie might want to crouch down a little more than in normal stance, to gain sight of the puck.

PLAN

This kind of situation leaves little time to play. If possible, the goalie should try to stop play; obviously, if there is traffic in front of the net, the goalie's team must be under pressure.

TRAINING EXERCISE

(7 to 9 minutes)

Screen shots can be difficult to practice with younger players. Safety is the issue. Young players have control problems with their shots — they have just learned to raise the puck and, impressed with their own skills, will raise the puck at all times. Consequently, players who stand in front of the net are sitting ducks.

Have only the coach or most accurate shooters shoot from the point, or restrict all shooters to wrist shots. *If you are not confident that this exercise will be safe, do not try it.*

Have one player stand in front of the net, at least two feet out from the crease, facing the shooter. This player tries to obstruct the goalie's view of the shot. Keep the shots slow at first, to help build the shooter's accuracy and the goalie's confidence.

Speed Variations

As goalies and shooters demonstrate confidence, increase the speed of shots and decrease the time between them. Also, add to the number of players in front of the crease. For example, try four: two defencemen trying to move two forwards out of the way.

SCREEN SHOTS

The first step for a goalie
is to locate the puck.

If eye contact is not established,
drop to Butterfly at the "sound"
of the shot.

CHECKLIST
For Screen Shots

☐ Goalie's first step: locate the puck.

☐ Goalie moves out of the net as far as possible, without losing sight of the puck and without becoming involved in the play.

☐ Goalie may crouch down a little more than usual.

☐ Goalie controls the rebound — either stops play or deflects the puck out of danger.

☐ Goalie stays up as long as possible.

☐ Shooters keep their shots low.

Shot Situation #5:

DEFLECTIONS

DEFINITION
A "deflection" is a shot that hits a player or stick on the way towards the net, thereby changing direction.

OPTIMUM POSITION
Goalies need to play high in the crease or even beyond it. They want to stay fairly close to the potential puck-deflector, to reduce the amount of net open to this player.

PLAN
This kind of situation leaves little time to play. If possible, the goalie should try to stop play. Obviously, if there is a player free to deflect the puck, the goalie must be under pressure.

TRAINING EXERCISE
(7 to 9 minutes)
Safety is a consideration in this exercise. Again, shots should be kept low and perhaps only wrist shots should be allowed. Players who cannot control their shots should not be allowed to take point shots. Again, do not use this drill if you are at all concerned about safety.

Have players line up inside the blueline, as far out from the net as you feel is useful. Each player takes a turn standing two to three feet in front of the crease, deflecting the shots of the other players.

Speed Variation
As goalies and shooters demonstrate more control, increase the speed of the shots and decrease the set-up time between shots.

DEFLECTIONS

The goalie needs to come out of the net and get close to the potential puck deflector.

CHECKLIST
For Deflections

☐ **Goalie's first step: locate the puck.**

☐ **Goalie moves to the top of the crease, fairly close to the puck-deflector.**

☐ **Goalie controls the rebound — either stops play or deflects the puck out of danger.**

☐ **Goalie stays up as long as possible.**

☐ **Shooters keep their shots low.**

Shot Situation #6:

PLAY COMING FROM BEHIND THE NET

DEFINITION
The puck starts out behind the net and is either carried or passed in front of the net.

OPTIMUM POSITION
The goalie should be right against the post nearest to the puck, with a skate touching this post. The stance should be fairly tight, with the goalie's body coming out at a forty-five degree angle from the goal line. Often, a goalie will hold the stick at the side of the net, parallel to the goal line, to block a centering pass. The goalie must watch the puck at all times but must never turn around to face it — the goalie's body must always be facing out front.

If players pass to someone in front of the net, the goalie pushes toward the puck, to cut down open net as quickly as possible. If players move to the front of the net on their own, the goalie maintains stance and stays on his or her feet.

You will often see players score after coming out from behind the net. The problem for goalies is that they must protect the near post and therefore cannot establish any backward motion to "skate with" the puck carrier. When players come around the net with the puck, goalies are, out of necessity, one step behind.

PLAN
Goalies are under pressure in this situation; if possible, they should stop play.

TRAINING EXERCISE
(8 to 10 minutes)
This exercise has three parts:

1. Form two lines, one at each face-off dot. One player starts at the face-off spot with the puck, skates behind the net and stops. The player from the other line takes position somewhere in the slot. The puck carrier passes to the player out front. Repeat until everyone has had at least one turn being the puck carrier.
2. Form one line on the right face-off circle. The player carries the puck behind the net from one side. The player may either stop or keep moving. In either case, the player skates out to the front of the net, the opposite side from which he or she started. The player may shoot at any point (a "wrap-around" or a slot shot). Once every player has had a shot, move to the left circle and repeat.
3. Form one line at the right face-off circle. Each player in turn carries the puck behind the net to the far side, stops, then moves quickly to the original side from which he or she came and takes a shot. Once everyone has had a turn, move to left circle and repeat.

Speed Variation
As all players demonstrate confidence, decrease set-up time between shots. Also, you might want to try this as a three-on-two exercise: three forwards against two defencemen.

PLAY FROM BEHIND THE NET

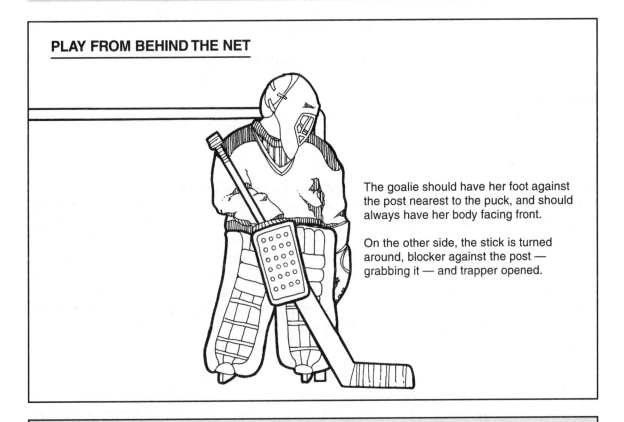

The goalie should have her foot against the post nearest to the puck, and should always have her body facing front.

On the other side, the stick is turned around, blocker against the post — grabbing it — and trapper opened.

CHECKLIST
For Play Coming from Behind the Net

☐ Goalie follows play but does not turn body towards the back of the net.

☐ Goalie maintains stance, with stick at the side of the net, blocking a centering pass.

☐ Goalie moves right up against the post nearest to the puck, with skate touching this post.

☐ If there is a pass, goalie moves directly towards the shooter.

☐ If goalie goes down, he or she gets back up right away.

☐ Ideally, goalie stops play.

Shot Situation #7:

TWO-ON-ONE

DEFINITION

A two-on-one occurs when two offensive players come in on one defensive player, usually the defenceman.

OPTIMUM POSITION

The two-on-one is an advanced situation, requiring a coordinated effort by the goalie and defenceman. The defenceman plays in front of, and halfway between, the puck carrier and the other forward as they cross the blueline. The defenceman wants to take away the puck-carrier's pass option. This means that if the puck carrier drives for the net, the defenceman is forced to play the skater and physically try to stop the puck carrier from crossing in front of the net.

The goalie is responsible for the puck carrier. In many ways this situation can be played like a breakaway, although the goalie has a much greater advantage here since the amount of ice available to the puck carrier is limited by the presence of the defenceman. If the puck carrier drives to the net, the goalie still plays the puck but must be wary of a pass to the open player.

The system breaks down when defencemen forget their role. They are not there to try to stop the shot (though that would be nice); they are there to take away the pass option from the puck carrier. On the other hand, they do not simply cover the open player, because they do not want to take themselves out of the play, thereby leaving too much open ice for the puck carrier.

There can also be a problem if the goalie is not aware of his or her role. The goalie must concentrate on the puck carrier and rely on the defencemen to do their job with the open player.

Communication is key to the two-on-one: goalie and defenceman must talk to each other as the play progresses.

PLAN

With two forwards bearing down, the goalie should stop play if possible, or at least direct the shot far away from the net.

TRAINING EXERCISE

(7 to 9 minutes)

Most coaches are familiar with the two-on-one drill. Form two groups: forwards and defence. Two forwards come in on one defenceman.

TWO-ON-ONES

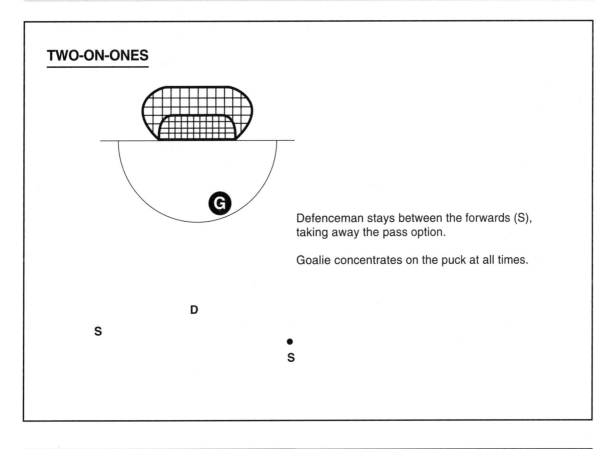

Defenceman stays between the forwards (S), taking away the pass option.

Goalie concentrates on the puck at all times.

CHECKLIST
For Two-on-Ones

☐ Defenceman plays in front of, and halfway between, forwards.

☐ Goalie plays the puck.

☐ Defenceman wants to take away the pass and will take out puck carrier if that player breaks for the net.

☐ Defenceman tries not to screen the goalie.

☐ Goalie and defenceman talk to each other.

☐ Goalie tries to stop play or directs puck out of danger.

PART TWO:
BEYOND THE FUNDAMENTALS

Kirk McLean making the save.

BEYOND THE FUNDAMENTALS

INTRODUCTION

Part 2 of *Behind The Mask* is designed to bring fundamentally sound goalies to a higher level of competence and performance. It's for goalies who have the desire to push themselves and for coaches who are committed to the development of their young goalies. Part 2 offers a complete coaching system: it shows you how to evaluate your goalies' performance and offers a series of drills that allow you to target weak areas of your goalies' game.

The instructions are simple and straightforward. The short Evaluation section will allow you to analyze your goalies' game quickly and easily. Then it's a matter of selecting the appropriate drills from the Skill Development section. The section called Proper Routine is designed to safely and effectively prepare your players for a game or practice. As in Part 1 (Mastering the Fundamentals), the drills incorporate other players as well as the goalie.

Patrick Roy.

TEACHING METHODS

The most important thing to remember when working with young goaltenders is that you are not practicing saves. A difficult save in a game is the result of pushing goalies to higher levels — and therefore missing saves — in practice. You should be concerned with three issues: fundamental play, conditioning and skill development.

1. FUNDAMENTAL PLAY

This refers to the building blocks of the goaltenders' game: stance, angles and motion. In all the drills in this book, it's essential for goalies to maintain sound fundamental play. It's the coach's job to help goalies keep the basics in mind. Any coach not familiar with the fundamentals should re-read Part 1 of *Behind The Mask*. Any goalie, of any age, without a keen understanding of stance, angles and motion is not ready for the advanced drills in this part of the book. They need to go back and learn the basics.

Key Concept: Coaches must ensure that their goalies maintain sound fundamental play throughout all drills. Goalies must strive to perfect these fundamentals.

2. CONDITIONING

From a goalie's point of view, conditioning refers to two things: cardiovascular fitness and upper-leg strength.

Often, you'll see goalies going down a lot in the third period or letting in a few "soft" goals late in the game. The problem is that they are either tired (physically), or lack the required focus (mentally). The constant up-and-down motion, combined with the weight of all that equipment, takes its toll, as do the pressures of a game.

It's important that coaches push their goalies towards that second effort in every drill. We recommend that you start every drill at a moderate pace, and build in intensity, which usually means you leave a shorter recovery period between shots and drill routines. You want your goalie not only to practice skills, but also to have an aerobic workout. A goalie who is in good shape is better able to cope with the physical and mental demands of a game.

Now, this doesn't mean we want you to push your goalies until they drop. Let them have a break to catch their breath and make sure they drink plenty of water. But they must get as good a workout as any other player on the ice.

Key Concept: Coaches must ensure that their goalies get a solid aerobic workout during practice. Leg strength and cardiovascular development is a given in all high-tempo drills.

3. SKILL DEVELOPMENT

The point of Part 2 is to help goalies become better at their position. This means that they will react faster and more effectively to shots and scoring situations as they come up during a game. There are three elements of skill development that the drills in this book focus on: speed (tempo), variety and repetition.

Speed

With each drill, we encourage you to start off slowly and gradually increase the speed of the shots or drill routines by decreasing the time between repetitions. You want to reach a point where the goalies are missing the save most of the time — the play is too fast. Stay at this level briefly, to force your goalies to work beyond their limits.

Key Concept: Forcing a goalie to do repetitions at a pace quicker than their capabilities will result in missed saves, but, in the long run, improves their reflexes.

Variety

Too often drills take a static situation and repeat it over and over. The problem is that during a game, unique situations come up again and again. The best strategy is to practice a wide variety of situations. We offer a variety of drills for each specific skill area to help practices reflect games as closely as possible. For example, most drills involve shooters who are constantly skating to allow the goalie to move or react as if in a game situation.

Key Concept: A "better" goalie is one who reacts faster to an ever-expanding range of drill situations.

Repetition

It is of no use to goaltenders if you do a drill once and then forget it, or move on to another drill. A goaltender can only develop if the shot or situation drill is repeated often (and even more often if it is a weak part of their game).

Key Concept: Repetition will improve goalies' play. Repetitive drill work is the responsibility of both the coach and the goaltender.

PLANNING YOUR PRACTICE

We recommend that you focus on only one drill, or two at the most, during a practice session. This implies, however, that you'll practice the skill well during the drill. Go over the Goal Evaluation Forms and look for a weak link in your goalies' game. Then you can target a series of drills to help your goalies work on this problem.

The amount of time you devote to your goalies is up to you. We hope that you find some time at every practice — more and more teams set aside practice time for goalies. In fact, we believe creative coaches can adapt what they learn from this book and make every practice drill and exercise a valuable experience for every player on the team, including the goalies.

And goalies — if your coach is not giving you reasonable attention at practice, you have every right to demand drill time. Remember, you will have a difficult time improving your skill level if you stand around or scrimmage all the time. Don't be a target — constantly try to improve.

Remember the key concepts: speed, variety and repetition!

THE IMPORTANCE OF PURPOSE

This is a book of drills designed to improve goaltenders' skills. To meet this end, it's important that the coach explain the purpose of each drill to the goalies before having them do it.

Learning sports skills is in part a conscious process. It's not enough just to do a drill without any explanation; in fact, many of these drills are similar — only differentiated by their intent. You must draw your goalies' attention to what they are supposed to be learning.

Each drill in this book starts off with a clear statement of purpose: always pass this statement along to your goalies.

And goalies — don't simply do the drills because you are told to by your coach. Ask questions until you are absolutely certain of the purpose of your hard work. It's easier to do drills well and with enthusiasm if you believe in what you are doing.

Evaluation

EVALUATING YOUR GOALIE'S ABILITIES

One of the most important things a coach can do for a developing player is to offer effective feedback. Some coaches, however, do not communicate with their goalies at all, while others merely say things like "good game" or "way to hang in there." Unfortunately, these coaches are not giving their goalies information which will help them to improve their skills.

The following Goal Evaluation Form allows the coach to keep a record of every goal scored in a game or scrimmage. This not only gives you a record of your goalies' performance, but of the entire team's play in a goal-against situation. After the game or scrimmage, the coach and goalies can review this form and decide which aspects of the goalies' game to work on in the next practice.

The form looks complicated at first, but it's very simple to use. We suggest you assign an assistant or parent to be "official record keeper." First of all, let's have a look at the form. Your assigned "statistician" should have a number of the forms ready before the game begins (feel free to photocopy this form for your own use), although it's easy enough to write up others as the game progresses.

GOAL EVALUATION FORM

1) Goalie: _____

2) Goal #: _____

3) Time: _____ Period: 1   2   3   OT

4) Situation: E   +   —   2o1   3o2   3o1   B

5) Net Zone: 1   2   3   4   5

6) Shot: L   R   W   SL   B   SN

7) Complication: P   S   D   R   X   PT

8) Goalie Motion: N   F   B   R   L

9) Goalie Position: F   K   S   D   B

10) Goalie Angle: H   L   C   OC

11) Comments: _____

_____

_____

12) Diagram

G = GOALIE
S = SHOOTER
Y = COMPLICATION
--- = PASS
—— = SHOT

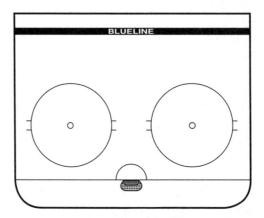

KEY TO THE GOAL EVALUATION FORM

1) Goalie
Most minor teams have more than one goalie; write the current goalie's name here.

2) Goal
Refers to the current number of goals against your team. If you are losing 3-0, it is goal #3.

3) Time & Period
Self explanatory.

4) Situation
Refers to your relative team strength:

E	=	even strength
+	=	power play advantage for your team (+2 would mean a two-player advantage)
—	=	a penalty killing disadvantage for your team (-2 means two players short)
2o1	=	two on one
3o1	=	three on one
3o2	=	three on two.
B	=	breakaway (B2 means a two-player breakaway).

5) Net Zone
The area of the net where the puck went in:

1 (high left)		2 (high right)
	5 (five-hole)	
3 (low left)		4 (low right)

6) Shot
Describes the shooter and the shot:

L	=	left-handed shooter
R	=	right-handed shooter
W	=	wrist shot
SL	=	slap shot
B	=	backhand shot
SN	=	snap shot

7) Complication
Describes the complicating circumstances in a goal:

P	=	a pass near the goal mouth
S	=	screen shot
D	=	deflection
R	=	a goal off a rebound
X	=	goalie came out of the net to play the shot
PT	=	point shot

8) Goalie Motion

Describes the goalie's motion at the time of the goal:

N = no motion
F = forward motion
B = backward motion
R = moving to the right
L = moving to the left

9) Goalie Position

Describes the goalie's position at the time of the goal:

F = on feet
K = on knees
S = doing the splits
D = down on the ice
B = butterfly

10) Goalie Angle

Describes the goalie's angle at the time of the goal:

H = high on the angle
L = low on the angle
C = on centreline
OC = off centre line

11) Comments

Self explanatory.

12) Diagram

As pictured, a schematic of the defensive zone, from outside the blueline to the back boards. This records several things:

G = the position of the goalie when the shot was taken
S = the position of the shooter when the shot was taken
Y = the position of the complicating factor
- - - = a pass or shot that changes directions
——— = the shot or deflection that results in a goal.

On the following pages, we have illustrated three sample situations.

GOAL EVALUATION FORM

1) Goalie: Jim Smith

2) Goal #: 1

3) Time: 1:05   **Period:** (1)   2   3   OT

4) Situation: (E)   +   —   2o1   3o2   3o1   B

5) Net Zone: 1   (2)   3   4   5

6) Shot: (L)   R   W   (SL)   B   SN

7) Complication: P   (S)   D   R   X   PT

8) Goalie Motion: (N)   F   B   R   L

9) Goalie Position: F   K   S   D   (B)

10) Goalie Angle: (H)   L   C   (OC)

11) Comments: too close to screen; off centreline

12) Diagram

G = GOALIE
S = SHOOTER
Y = COMPLICATION
--- = PASS
—— = SHOT

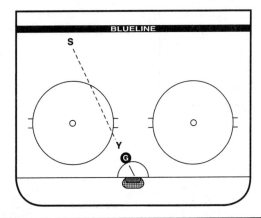

GOAL EVALUATION FORM

1) Goalie: Jim Smith

2) Goal #: 2

3) Time: 18:29   **Period:** 1   (**2**)   3   OT

4) Situation: (**E**)   +   —   2o1   3o2   3o1   B

5) Net Zone: 1   2   3   (**4**)   5

6) Shot: L   (**R**)   W   SL   B   (**SN**)

7) Complication: P   S   (**D**)   R   X   PT

8) Goalie Motion: (**N**)   F   B   R   L

9) Goalie Position: (**F**)   K   S   D   B

10) Goalie Angle: H   (**L**)   C   (**OC**)

11) Comments: played shooter
stayed deep recognizing pass opportunity to open man in front

12) Diagram

G = GOALIE
S = SHOOTER
Y = COMPLICATION
--- = PASS
—— = SHOT

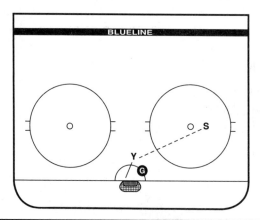

GOAL EVALUATION FORM

1) Goalie: Jim Smith

2) Goal #: 3

3) Time: 19:08   **Period:** 1   (2)   3   OT

4) Situation: E   +   (—1)   2o1   3o2   3o1   B

5) Net Zone: 1   2   3   (4)   5

6) Shot: L   (R)   (W)   SL   B   SN

7) Complication: (P)   S   D   R   X   PT

8) Goalie Motion: N   F   B   (R)   L

9) Goalie Position: (F)   K   S   D   B

10) Goalie Angle: H   (L)   C   (OC)

11) Comments: did not watch puck behind net
got caught out of position for centering pass

12) Diagram

G = GOALIE
S = SHOOTER
Y = COMPLICATION
--- = PASS
—— = SHOT

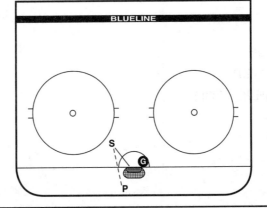

PROPER ROUTINE

WARM-UP

Ask goalies what their least favourite part of hockey is, and most will answer: warm-up! Sadly, there are few goalies who haven't been injured by a shot during warm-up. It's a ridiculous situation — can you imagine a football quarterback being pulled moments before a big game because he was injured during the warm-up?

The warm-up is supposed to be a transitional period, bridging the gap between inactivity and extreme physical exertion. Its purpose is to limber up the muscles, get the blood flowing, and help the goalies get a "feel" for the puck. But perhaps the most important aspect of the warm-up is mental, as a game requires concentration and focus.

Unfortunately, most warm-ups are examples of anarchy in motion. Players drill the puck haphazardly but as hard as they can at the goalie, hoping to score. It's the coach's job to ensure that all players understand their roles as soon as they hit the ice. This means that even the pre-game warm-up should be organized and purposeful.

A NOTE ON STRETCHING

Most sports doctors and trainers recommend that athletes stretch before and after an activity to cut the risk of muscle damage.

We encourage goalies to follow a systematic stretching routine and to incorporate it into their warm-up for both practices and games, paying special attention to the groin area. There are many guidebooks and pamphlets available on stretching, so we won't go into it in any detail. One tip: the best way to start any on-ice session is with a light skate, and remember — lots of water throughout.

For practice, an ideal routine — although it's not always possible — would look something like this:

- stretching, off and on the ice
- light skate
- warm-up drill
- skill-building drill
- light skate

Excellent Overall Drill

THE CONTROLLED SHOT DRILL

This drill provides an effective practice for most of the team, taking into account the special needs of the goalies. It takes into consideration all of the specific skill drills outlined in the sections to follow. Remember that the pace can set the tone for the entire practice. Your aim is to have a disciplined and purposeful practice that prepares the players to go to the next level.

PURPOSE

To attain a moderate level of physical activity for all players, and to take control of the players and focus their attention. This drill will give the goalies a complete set of movements that develop skating skills and angles.

DRILL DESCRIPTION

This is an organized drill based on typical game situations. This is an important drill for shooters as well as goalies. The emphasis is on control of shooting, passing and skating. This drill has six parts.

Part 1: Stationary Shots — Long Range

The coach has the players line up between the blueline and the top of the face-off circle, spread out across the ice, facing the net; a couple of players or assistants may be near the net to retrieve pucks.

One by one, moving through the line in order from one side to the other, the players shoot at the goalie. Have the shooters keep the shots low and controlled. After a few rotations, reduce the time between shooters to force goalies to work a little harder. Remind your shooters that they are not trying to score; they are warming up their goalies and gaining control over their shot.

Part 2: Adding Motion — Shots from the Wing

By now your goalies should be loosened up. It's time to add motion to the shooters' routine. Form two lines, one at each end of the blueline, facing the net. Players skate to the top of the face-off circle and then shoot; do not allow shots above the waist.

Alternate shots from each line, and gradually decrease the time between shooters until the next player goes immediately after the previous player's shot has been taken. By now, everyone is starting to work a little harder and the goalie is forced to move laterally at a very high pace.

Part 3: Stationary Shots — Close In

Have the team form two lines at the top of the face-off circle. Alternate shots from each side.

Part 4: Wing Breakaways

Have two lines at each end of the blueline. The shooters carry the puck down their wing and cut across the slot for a close-in shot. Alternate sides, with the next player starting as soon as the preceding player has taken a shot.

Part 5: Two-on-Os or Two-on-Ones

Again, start with two lines at each side of the blueline. A player from each line moves in on the goalie — a two person breakaway. Limit the passing to three passes, maximum.

Don't allow your goalies to cheat — they must follow the puck carrier as passes are made. Remember, you are not looking for saves. You are looking for everyone to be skating harder and concentrating.

If you want to include your defence now, you could introduce them to create a two-on-one.

Part 6: Centre Breakaways

Shooters come in from the blueline and shoot or deke. They start on the whistle, regardless of whether or not the goalie is ready. For example, on the whistle, shooter #1 skates in and dekes the goalie. While the goalie is down from the deke, start the next shooter. This forces the goalie up and out for the next breakaway. This is a magnificent conditioner.

COACH'S JOB

Make it your goal to never have a player injured during these practice drills. This means that, after stretching, all players should start off fairly slowly and gradually build up their intensity. It also means that shooters should keep their shots under control.

Note: This drill requires one end of the rink from the blueline in, and takes about 30 minutes. Your goalies cannot get a better technical and physical workout.

SKILL DEVELOPMENT DRILLS
Skating

You often hear sports commentators talk about how great the goaltenders were in the old days. They speculate on how Original Six goalies like Jacques Plante, Glenn Hall, Terry Sawchuk and Johnny Bower would dominate the NHL today.

The game of hockey has changed a lot over the last twenty years. Today's players are bigger, faster, and generally shoot much harder than in the "old days." Previously, players would skate up and down their wings in a predictable way. Now, there is an intricate system of crisscross plays, drop-passes, and giant wingers barrelling into the goal area. As great as they were in their day, the goalies of old would likely feel out of place in today's NHL.

The reason is simple: skating.

Goalies of old were encouraged to "stand up," and to never wander from their crease. Although some old-time goalies were great skaters, it wasn't considered an important part of their game. Things have changed. Skating is the single most important skill of the modern goaltender. A goalie has to be able to challenge shooters, and keep up with the rapid shifts in the flow of the game. The following drills are designed to help goalies' skating, both laterally (side-to-side) and vertically (forward and backward).

The good news is that while reflexes and attitude are harder to teach goalies, skating can improve with the most basic efforts. There are a few simple drills here, but you will see a rapid improvement in your goalies' play if you use these drills on a regular basis.

Martin Brodeur plays the puck.

Skating Drill #1

FORWARD & BACKWARD MOTION

PURPOSE

To improve goalies' ability to follow the play as it moves towards and away from the goal line, while constantly maintaining a proper angle.

DRILL DESCRIPTION — Part One

Shooters (6 to 8) line up at centre ice. On your whistle, one at a time, they break in on the goalie and shoot — without any dekes — before reaching the hash marks. Start with shooters coming directly in from the centre-ice circle. Later, have them come in from the wings, but do not let them cut across to the other side.

Goalies starts in crease. On the whistle, goalies move out to the "ready" position, at least 10 feet in front of the crease. Instruct them to slowly move backwards as the shooter approaches. They want to make the save before they are in the crease. On the whistle, they must quickly make their way 10 feet beyond the crease again, to face the next shooter.

DRILL DESCRIPTION — Part Two

Same drill but start shooters at the blueline, not at centre.

**Forward & Backward Motion
Centre Shots**

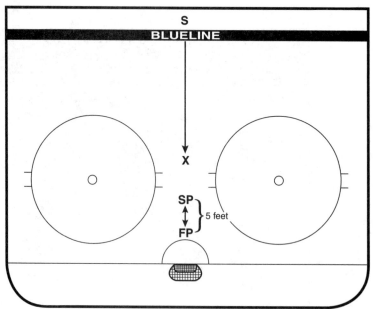

SP = Starting Point   X = Shot Point
FP = Finishing Point   S = Shooter

Variations

The first time you do this drill, start with the goalies standing still at the top of the crease. Goalies will probably be scored on, but that's okay. With their feet still, it is difficult for goalies to quickly move into a low shot or a deke. Explain to the goalies that you want to show them the importance of motion and angles. To understand these concepts, they first have to see how ineffective it is to simply stand still. After a few minutes with them standing still, proceed with the normal drill.

Goalies must come out quickly, and then move backwards slowly and smoothly, maintaining proper stance and angle. As the goalies move back, they should keep in mind the centre line and telescoping concepts as noted in Part 1. On the whistle, goalies must immediately return to the "ready" position. If a shot beats a goalie, look at two things:

- Where did the goalie finish in relation to the crease?
- What was the goalie's centre-line position?

COACH'S JOB

Watch that the goalies maintain proper stance. Also, make sure the goalies don't "cheat" by staying too close to the net — they should quickly move at least 10 feet beyond the crease. As the drill progresses, decrease the time between shooters (i.e. have shooters start on the whistle, and blow the whistle at shorter intervals). The coach should always dictate the pace of the drill, not the players.

Always remember that the purpose of this drill is to improve your goalies' forward-backward motion. Because shooting is involved, the angles are extremely important.

Note: The faster the pace, the greater the goalies' skating requirements and improvement.

Skating Drill #2

LATERAL MOTION

PURPOSE

To improve the goalies' ability to follow the play as it moves from side to side across the ice, using the Shuffle and T-Push.

DRILL DESCRIPTION — Shuffle

Shooters line up on the blueline, right or left side. On the whistle they skate down one wing, then cut across to the other side before the face-off circle hash marks. They may shoot at any time as they cut across, but they are not to go to the net and try to deke.

Goalies start out in the crease. On your whistle, they come at least 10 feet out of their crease, to the "ready" position. The goalie moves backwards as the play comes to the net, always maintaining a high angle (i.e. taking away the shot). As the shooter crosses at the hash marks, the goalie commences the Shuffle and always maintains a high position (outside the crease) and a proper centre-line on the puck.

Shuffle Drill

SP = Starting Point
FP = Finishing Point
X = Shot Point
S = Shooter

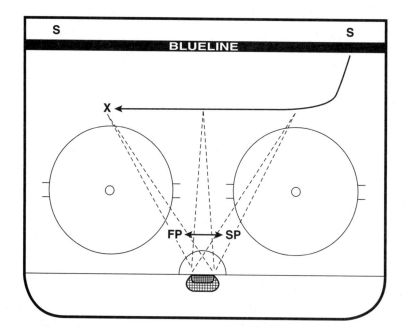

DRILL DESCRIPTION — T-Push

Once the goalies are warmed up, allow the shooters to cut deep after the hash marks. This is when goalies can practice the T-Push. As with the Shuffle, the goalies start high and take the shot away as they move backwards when the shooter drives deep across the net. Rather than poke-check, the goalies transfer to the T-Push, using the backwards motion to flow into the T. The goalies try to keep a proper angle and hold their feet all the way across the net. At all times, the space in the Five-Hole is minimized.

Shooters line up on the blueline, right or left side. On the whistle, they skate through the dot of the circle and drive across the top of the crease (i.e. deep), carrying the puck across and trying to stuff the Five-Hole.

Goalies should come out quickly and high; flow backwards, maintaining a proper angle; and then move sideways quickly and smoothly as the player skates across. It is very important that goalies remain on their feet as they move to the side and make the save. On the whistle they must quickly regain the ready position.

T-Push Drill

SP = Starting Point
FP = Finishing Point
X = Shot Point
S = Shooter

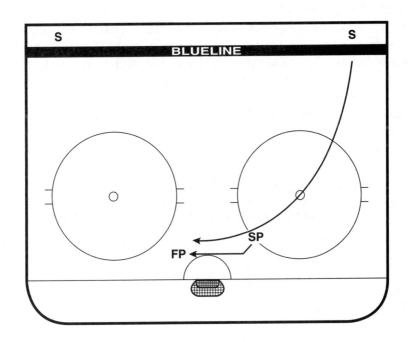

Variation
Alternate left and right side. For example, a right winger drives across the net, right to left. The goalie finishes on the left-wing side, then the left winger drives in, finishing on the right side.

COACH'S JOB — Shuffle and T-Push
Watch that goalies maintain proper stance, keep an appropriate angle, use motion to their advantage and do not drop down to the ice. You want them to cut cleanly, and not back into the crease. This is a drill to develop your goalies' lateral motion. No poke-checks please.

Note: For lateral motion when the play is close to the net, goalies use the T-Push style of skating. Goalies should use the T-Push in this drill. For a further description of the T-Push, see Part 1 of this book, pages 23-24.

Skating Drill #3

LATERAL MOTION WITH PLAY FURTHER OUT

PURPOSE

To improve the goalies' ability to follow the play as the puck moves from side to side across the ice, using the Shuffle skating method.

DRILL DESCRIPTION

Position two shooters at the top of each circle. The goalie, in a proper stance (i.e. standing still), faces the puckholder. The puckholder passes to the other winger who will shoot, forcing the goalie to "shuffle" over to make the save. The higher the goalies start, the further across they must go. This is good. There are two solid points:

1. The goalie must cross using the shuffle from a standing position, which is very difficult.
2. The faster the pass, the quicker the goalie must move.

Note: Because the goalies are starting from a standing position, a "crossover" move is very effective. Simply cross one pad over the other in the direction you want to go, and hop over. It won't be pretty to watch but it gets you there!

LEG STRENGTH

Goalies' upper leg muscles get more work than any other part of their body. The weight of the pads, the constant up and down motion, even proper stance — all these wear down the upper legs during the course of a game or practice. It's important, then, that goalies build up their leg muscles. What they want to achieve is a combination of strength, flexibility and durability.

Serious goalies will develop an off-ice routine of their own. A suitable routine would include both weight training and stretching. Kids who are interested in such a routine should talk to the trainer at their local health club, recreation centre or YM-YWCA.

Coaches can also help goalies build up their leg muscles. Here are three simple on-ice drills that work your goalies' legs.

Note: As you've probably realized, every drill we do works the legs. But if you have time in your workouts, or your goalies need extra leg-strength work, these are excellent drills.

Ron Hextall controls the puck.

Leg Strength Drill #1

BUTTERFLY

PURPOSE

To build upper leg strength, while practicing the proper Butterfly save technique.

DRILL DESCRIPTION

Coach or assistant works with goalies on their own. Goalies stand at goal line, facing the boards (away from other players). On the whistle, they skate backwards slowly and smoothly, maintaining stance as if they are facing a shooter. On the coach's signal, they drop down to their knees in the butterfly position:

- knees close together
- feet splayed
- stick blade on the ice and at the knees
- trapper out and open
- body upright

Goalies return to their feet immediately, continue to the blueline, then turn around and work their way back to the boards.

Goalie Objective

Goalies must return to their feet quickly, regaining backward motion and stance.

COACH'S JOB

Watch for proper motion, stance and a quick return to feet. The faster the coach's whistles, the faster the goalies will be forced to their feet. This drill should be tiring, with many repetitions creating the desired result.

Note: This drill can also be done in the stance while skating forward. Goalies should be able to drop to the butterfly as they challenge the shooter — not all shots are taken when a goalie's motion is backwards. Goalies will find this to be a great cardiovascular workout.

Leg Strength Drill #2

RAPID FIRE — BUTTERFLY

PURPOSE
To build upper leg strength, while practicing the proper butterfly save technique.

DRILL DESCRIPTION
Form one line of shooters — say five — per goalie. Shooters start at the blueline, while goalies start five feet inside the blueline, facing the shooters. Goalies start backwards motion in their proper stance. On your whistle, shooters skate towards the goalie, taking one hard, low shot after another. Each shooter will peel off after the shot, going to the back of the line.

Goalies drop to the butterfly, make the save, then quickly regain their feet, motion and stance, and continue backwards motion. Continue until all the shooters are done. Return to the blueline and do it again. Starting from the blueline and skating backwards is the natural direction for a goalie.

Goalie Objective
Goalies must return to their feet quickly, regaining backward motion and stance while exercising extreme concentration.

COACH'S JOB
Watch for proper motion, stance, and a quick return to feet. Make sure shooters direct their shots towards the goalies' legs, thereby forcing the quick butterfly.

Note: The harder the shot, the faster the goalie has to move. Remember, we're not looking for saves, but rather for effort and quickness. The goalies' upper legs and wind will again receive a great workout.

Leg Strength Drill #3

REBOUNDS

PURPOSE

Goalies practice getting up to their feet quickly.

DRILL DESCRIPTION

If you have two goalies, divide the group in two and use both ends. Shooters line up at the top of the face-off area, in a semi-circle in front of the goalie. Each shooter has as many pucks as possible, to keep the drill going.

On your whistle, goalies face each shooter and drop to their knees, face the shot, and return to their feet right away. The shot should come while goalies are going down. Move through the semi-circle in order, with each shooter taking one shot at a time. As the drill progresses, decrease time between shots, making effective use of the whistle.

Goalie Objective

Goalies must return to their feet quickly, regaining proper stance while concentrating on the shot.

COACH'S JOB

Watch for proper motion, stance, and a quick return to feet (the most important aspect). Make sure the shots are hard, forcing the goalies to perform the drill more quickly.

STANCE

"Stance" refers to the way goalies position their bodies in preparation for a shot. Stance can be a difficult concept for a coach to pass on to goalies because it is rather idiosyncratic. In time, all goalies develop their own stance, but there are elements common to every successful stance.

We will get to these elements in a moment, but first a word about style. We often hear debates about what "style" of stance is the most effective, and generally there are two camps: those who favour the "stand-up" style, and those who favor the "butterfly" style.

Stand-up goalies keep their feet close together and their legs and bodies fairly upright. They rarely go down to the ice to make a save. Johnny Bower, Jacques Plante, Gerry Cheevers, Bernie Parent — all are considered great stand-up goalies.

With the butterfly style, goalies keep their feet spread wide apart, bend their legs at the knee, and crouch down. Butterfly goalies drop down to their knees frequently in order to make a save. Classic butterfly goalies include Glenn Hall and Tony Esposito.

The butterfly style was a development of the late 1960s and early 1970s. Goalies found that in the post-Bobby Hull world of hockey, slapshots and curved sticks were the norm. The old stand-up style left the bottom corners of the net easy pickings for these faster shooters.

Where do we stand on style?

Well, just to add more fuel to the fire, we don't think that either classic style is effective for today's goalies. Just as the butterfly style was an attempt to adapt to the changing face of hockey, today's goalies need a style that is best suited to the modern game. Today's players are bigger, faster and stronger, and there is much more lateral motion.

The style we recommend is called the "Inverted-V" style, and features elements of both the stand-up and butterfly styles.

We cover the Inverted-V Style extensively in Part 1 of this book. The main element — the key to every style — is the position of the feet and legs. The ideal stance is with knees together, slightly bent, and the feet apart, forming an Inverted-V pattern. This stance readies goalies for all kinds of circumstances: low shots, high shots, screen shots, side-to-side movement. Note that this style defies the common wisdom about stance — the belief that goalies should keep their legs together at all times.

We also defy another "old coach's tale." We often hear TV commentators advising young goalies to never drop down to the ice. But the problem isn't with goalies who drop down, it's with goalies who don't get up again quickly. That's why we spend so much time working on the upper legs and on cardiovascular conditioning. In the modern game, goalies who can regain position quickly have the upper hand.

The drills in this section are designed to overcome bad habits your goalies may have picked up. The most helpful thing that you can do as a coach is to become aware of the elements of effective stance, and constantly remind your goalies when they lapse in a certain area. To help you identify these important points, consult the Stance Checklist for the Inverted-V Style, which appears on page 20 in Part 1.

Stance Drill

PURPOSE
This drill is not for every goalie. It's for those who are devoted to an outdated style (a goalie who perhaps was influenced by an old-fashioned coach or parent). This drill is designed to demonstrate the advantages and limitations of the stand-up, butterfly and Inverted-V styles.

DRILL DESCRIPTION
Line up shooters on the blueline. Start off with goalies in the stand-up style: feet close together, body upright. On your whistle, have shooters move in on goal; they may shoot or deke. Let the shooters know that the low corners are particularly vulnerable with this kind of style.

Next, have the goalies switch to an exaggerated butterfly style: feet well apart, knees apart, and knees and body bent. Goalies start off at the top of the crease. On your whistle, shooters move in on goal with an eye to shooting at the vulnerable Five-Hole, and may shoot or deke. In this style, the most obvious open shooting area is the Five-Hole.

Finally, have your goalies line up in the Inverted-V: knees together, feet slightly apart. On your whistle, shooters move in. Goalies start 10 feet outside the crease and flow back as the shooter approaches.

Goalie Objective
Goalies must test each style to know which style is most comfortable and offers the greatest number of moves for each shot.

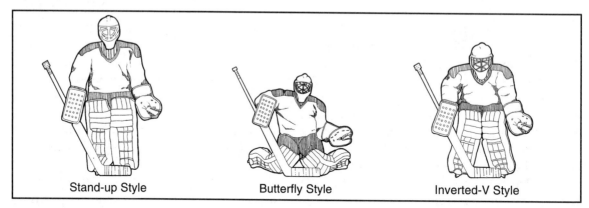

Stand-up Style   Butterfly Style   Inverted-V Style

COACH'S JOB
Make the point of this drill clear to the goalies. In all likelihood, the Inverted-V Style will result in the fewest goals, so after the drill make sure that this conclusion is clear.

CONCLUSION
The goalies should feel that, with the stand-up style, low shots are difficult and dekes result in lunging movements. In the butterfly style, the knees must drop quickly to cover the Five-Hole and lunging is required for dekes. In the Inverted-V Style with motion, Five-Hole goals are minimized — because there's less room to shoot — and motion allows the goalies to drop to their knees and easily play dekes. In both the butterfly and Inverted-V Style, low shots are easier to save.

ANGLES

Old-time goalies really understood the concept of "angles." It's a simple idea. If goalies draw an imaginary line from the point where a shot is taken to the middle of the goal line, and then position themselves along this imaginary line, they will be in the best place to make a save.

In Part 1, we broke down "playing the angles" into three components:

1. Goalies establish their position in the net.
2. Goalies approximate their optimum position for making a save (also called "telescoping").
3. Goalies move to that position.

The best way for goalies to learn about angles is to have them face a lot of shots. It really is a trial and error process. We've included a couple of drills here. They're designed to reinforce the key concept in "playing the angles": that goalies position themselves along an imaginary line running from the point where the shot is taken to the centre of the goal line. The higher the goalie is along this line, the better the angle will be. For example, if a goalie starts off on the centre line deep in the net, an opening will exist; as the goalie moves closer to the puck, less of this opening will show.

Angle Drill #1

WITH MOTION

PURPOSE

To reinforce the key concept that goalies position themselves along an imaginary line running from the point where the shot is taken to the centre of the goal line.

DRILL DESCRIPTION

Shooters start at the centre red line in two rows. Alternating between rows, shooters approach the goal on the whistle. Shooters must stay on their wings or go straight up the centre, and must shoot from 20 to 25 feet from the net.

Goalies start off in back of crease, at the very centre of the goal line. As the shooter begins, the goalies quickly move well out of the crease and directly towards the puck. Once goalies reach this optimum position, they adopt proper stance and begin to move backwards slowly and smoothly. Once the save is made, goalies regain their original position at the middle of the goal line.

As the drill progresses, decrease the time between shooters.

Goalie Objective

Goalies must quickly gain centre line positioning, then quickly return to starting point after save is made.

COACH'S JOB

First, make it clear to your goalies that this is a training exercise to teach them about angles. They would not play a real game breakaway by starting in the back of their crease.

Watch that goalies are playing the angles properly. A common problem is that goalies play the shooter instead of the puck. This leaves them improperly lined up for the angle.

Angle Drill #2

RAPID FIRE

PURPOSE

To reinforce the concept that goalies position themselves along an imaginary line running from the point where the shot is taken to the centre of the goal line.

DRILL DESCRIPTION

Shooters form a semi-circle at the top of the face-off areas. Shooters have as many pucks as possible. Goalies start off in the crease, in the middle of the goal line. Goalies move to optimum position on the designated shooter — have shooters shoot in a logical order so goalies know where to go. Goalies should be at least five feet out of the crease. Once they reach that position, they establish stance and begin moving backwards slowly. On the whistle, the shooter shoots. Once goalies make the save, they must quickly return to their starting position.

Note: It is very helpful for goalies to "tap" the short-side posts for shots from the wings. This simple move guarantees centre-line accuracy on the angle.

Variation

Move shooters progressively closer to give goalies a quick reaction challenge. Decrease time between shooters.

Goalie Objective

Goalies must quickly gain optimum position. After the save, they must quickly regain starting position.

COACH'S JOB

Again, remind goalies that this is a training exercise. Also, watch that they line up properly — on the puck, not the shooter.

Angle Drill: Rapid Fire

SP = Starting Point
FP = Finishing Point
S = Shooter
G = Goalie

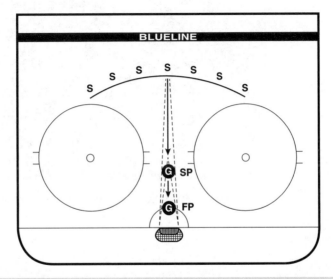

REBOUNDS

This section looks at two aspects of rebounds: control and recovery. First, we offer a comprehensive drill to help goalies control rebounds. This is followed by two drills that work on the most common types of rebound situations.

Remember, a key to controlling rebounds is that goalies must establish and maintain a smooth and steady backwards motion. This helps draw the puck towards goalies after they make the save.

Martin Brodeur preparing for a rebound.

Rebound Drill #1

CONTROLLING REBOUNDS

PURPOSE
To systematically work through goalies' save repertoire, concentrating on techniques which avoid giving rebounds.

DRILL DESCRIPTION
Shooters line up just outside the hash marks in a semi-circle. Goalies start a few feet beyond the crease. Leave enough time between shots for the goalies to get into position. They must establish a backwards motion before the shot is taken. It is this motion that helps goalies cushion shots and reduce the chance of a rebound.

Goalie Objective
Goalies must establish ready position quickly, and establish and maintain a backwards motion. They must use the backwards motion to control rebounds, quickly drawing the puck towards their bodies if a rebound gets away, or slapping the rebound into the corner. This is also a mental conditioning process, necessary for the goalie who must always be aware of rebound requirements.

COACH'S JOB
Make sure goalies establish and maintain backwards motion, and quickly fall on or redirect any rebounds that do get away. Keep everyone focused on the purpose: to help goalies learn how to control rebounds.

Rebound Drill #2

CONTROL DRILL WITH MOTION

PURPOSE

Many rebounds come from the leg pads. This drill works on controlling these kinds of rebounds, with an emphasis on the important backwards motion.

DRILL DESCRIPTION

Goalies start on the blueline, facing the far-end boards. If you are working with two goalies, have them at each end of the blueline. Shooters are lined up on the centre line, facing goalies.

Goalies establish backwards motion, maintaining stance. On your whistle, a shooter skates towards the goalie, shooting hard at the leg pads. Goalies drop down to make the save and control the rebound, then regain feet and start backwards motion again. Shooters continue to fire low until the goalies reach the back boards. Reposition the goalies and shooters like they were at the start of the drill, and repeat. Try to get at least five hard, low shots per drill.

Goalie Objective

Goalies must establish and maintain stance and motion. They must regain feet immediately and continue backwards motion. This is excellent for butterfly practice, and, if practiced faithfully, produces excellent rebound control habits.

COACH'S JOB

Make sure the shooters are on target: shots to the leg pads only. Watch that your goalies maintain backwards motion and regain feet quickly. Allow them enough time to cover rebounds and regain feet, but keep them working at a steady pace.

Rebound Drill #3

RECOVERING FROM CLOSE-IN REBOUNDS

PURPOSE
Rebounds that fall close to the net are the most dangerous. Usually goalies are down and out of the play, and must recover. This is a drill designed to practice this dangerous — but common — situation.

DRILL DESCRIPTION
Only a few shooters are needed for this drill. Goalies face shooter. On whistle, goalies drop to knees and shooter shoots. This forces goalies to concentrate on shots and get to their feet fast. Do not wait for goalies to be set — the opposition doesn't.

Note: The further away the shooters are, the easier the drill.

Variation — Rebound-to-Side
Not all rebounds are straight ahead. Position shooters to the right or left of goalies. When the goalies drop, shots will be from the side, forcing the goalies to quickly move laterally for a save.

Variation — Two-Pad Stack
Start with goalies on their sides, as if they've just made a two-pad stack. This can be done from a stationary two-pad stack or with motion into a two-pad stack. In either case, the whistle blows as skates hit the goal posts.

Note: Again, saves are not the important aspect of this drill. The effort and rapidity of recovery will eventually result in saves. Goalies must strive to achieve greater levels of performance.

Rebound-to-Side Drill

G = Goalie
S = Shooter

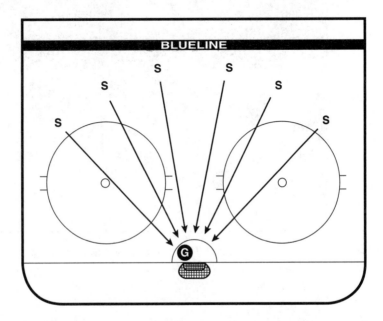

PLANNING
The "One Step Ahead" Concept

Goalies should never make a save out of context. This means that they should never think of merely stopping the puck — although in desperate situations, that's the best you can hope for. But in most cases goalies should have a plan: they've made the save, now what?

To complete a routine save, goalies have two simple options: stop play or continue play.

When do goalies want to stop play?
• When their team is under pressure, or when there are opposition players near the goal.

How do goalies stop play?
• By holding the puck, falling on top of it, or deflecting it out of play.

Goalies want to continue play — when their team is not under pressure — by deflecting or passing the puck to a teammate who is not under pressure from an opposition player.

Patrick Roy considers his next play.

Planning Drill #1

FOCUSED SHOTS AND RESPONSE

PURPOSE

To systematically work through goalies' save repertoire, concentrating on techniques which avoid leaving rebounds and properly finish the save. This is a natural follow-up to the rebound drills.

DRILL DESCRIPTION

Shooters line up at blueline. With each shot, the goalies either:
- prevent the rebound by freezing the puck
- redirect the shot to corner, out of danger

Goalies start a few feet beyond the crease. Leave enough time between shots for them to get into position. They can stand still or use a backwards motion before the shot is taken. The motion helps goalies cushion shots and reduce the chance of a rebound. Also, tell your goalies to have a plan to follow for each section of the drill: either they want to continue or to stop play. A save is not complete until their plan has been realized.

Have two players behind the nets and to the sides to retrieve pucks, and to act as "open players" when goalies are continuing the play.

Goalie Objective

Goalie must establish ready position quickly, establish and maintain stance, and initiate backwards motion. They should use the backwards motion to control rebounds. Goalies must be aware of what they are trying to do.

COACH'S JOB

Make sure goalies know their plan and finish the save. Make sure your shooters stay on target.

DEFLECTIONS

Today's goalies have to contend with a lot of traffic around their nets. In a game, it's likely that many of the shots goalies face are either screened or deflected. Deflections are particularly difficult because the puck instantly changes direction — often leaving goalies high and dry. Therefore, positioning is the key to effectively playing deflections. There are four elements to what we call "optimum position":

1. Goalies are able to see the puck.
2. Goalies are high in the crease or outside of it.
3. Goalies move close to the puck deflector.
4. Goalies stay on their feet for as long as possible.

There are two other important points:

1. Goalies should not be content with playing deep in their crease, thus relying only on reflexes; deflections happen too fast.
2. Goalies should take quick glances around the net and be aware of all deflection possibilities.

Deflection Drill #1

POSITIONING

PURPOSE
To develop goalies' concept of "good position." Make sure that goalies play the shooter and react to the deflection by moving to the point of deflection.

DRILL DESCRIPTION
Three skaters are needed for this drill. Have one skater at each point: these are the "point shooters." Have the third skater in front of the net: this is the "puck deflector."

On your whistle, the point shooters take shots from a stationary position. The shooters alternate from left point to right point. The player in front of the net tries to deflect these shots. Make sure your shooters are accurate and keep their shots low. Decrease the time between shots as the drill progresses.

Goalie Objective
Goalies start in crease, then move to point of deflection as shot is taken. The aim is for goalies to be aware of the possibility of a deflection and to move to block the shot, and not try to make the save on reflex.

COACH'S JOB
Make sure that goalies understand and employ the four elements of optimum position. Make sure the shooters keep their shots low.

Variation
As your goalies become adept in this drill, have the point shooters pass the puck back and forth before taking the shot. As well, you could add another deflector, giving the shooter an option.

Stationary Deflection Drill

S = Shooter
D = Deflector
G = Goalie

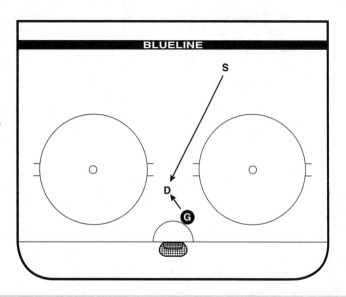

Deflection Drill #2

POINT DEFLECTIONS

PURPOSE
To practice recovering position from deflections that catch goalies well out of the play.

DRILL DESCRIPTION
Position shooter at the point and deflector in the centre just inside the blueline. On your whistle, the deflector drives to the slot to redirect the point shot.

Goalies start about five feet outside the crease, in line with shooter, and slowly start moving backwards. When the shot goes to the middle, goalies use this backwards movement to achieve maximum angle position at point of deflection.

Goalie Objective
Goalie must practice a backwards motion across to the deflector, trying to keep positioned in a proper angle and on their feet. It is essential that goalies be aware of the possibility of deflection.

COACH'S JOB
To watch that a low feed comes from the stationary shooter, and to see that the goalies move smoothly backwards and across to the deflector.

Point Deflection Drill

S = Shooter
D = Deflector
PD = Point of Deflection
G = Goalie

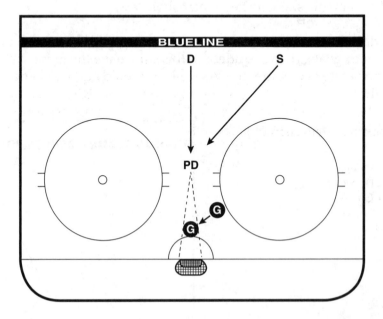

Deflection Drill #3

SLOT DEFLECTIONS

PURPOSE
Not all deflections are from close range. With shots from the point and with little traffic directly in front of the net, goalies must still be ready for the puck to change direction.

DRILL DESCRIPTION
Again, three or four players are all that you need. Have shooters on each point, plus one deflector positioned in the slot at least 10 feet out from the goal line.

On your whistle, goalies move to ready position to face the point shot. The player at the point shoots a low hard shot for the player in the slot to deflect. In this situation, goalies are in the crease and come to the deflector.

Note: Goalies should never leave a possible deflector behind them. If a deflector is positioned at the side, the goalie must play deeper.

Variation
Have two players spread out so that one is in the slot, the other to the side of the crease.

Goalie Objective
Goalies must establish ready position quickly and reach for the deflector.

COACH'S JOB
Make sure goalies move quickly to ready position. Don't let them cheat by leaning in advance towards the deflector. Make sure the point shots are low.

Note: By coming as close to the point of the deflection as possible (and staying on their feet), goalies will cause any uncontrolled rebound to bounce away from the deflector, hopefully avoiding an immediate rebound.

SCREEN SHOTS

As we said in the last section, modern goalies spend most of the game with their view of the puck partially or completely obscured. Once again, "optimum position" is the key to an effective defence against screen shots. Here are the elements that will lead goalies to their optimum position in the screen shot situation:

- Goalies must try to see the puck at all times.
- Goalies either:
a) come out of the net as far as possible, without losing sight of the play and without becoming involved in the play, in order to create an angle; or
b) drop deeper in their crease, trying to get sight of the puck.
- Goalies may crouch down a little more than usual (i.e. look around and through the legs rather than the bodies of players).

The following three drills will help develop goalies' ability to effectively play screen shots.

Trevor Kidd handles a screen shot.

Screen Shot Drill #1

POSITION

PURPOSE

To develop goalies' concept of "good position" on a screen shot.

DRILL DESCRIPTION

You need only a few skaters for this drill. Have one skater in each blueline face-off area — these are the "point shooters." Have a third skater in front of the net — this is the "screen." On your whistle, the point shooters take shots from a stationary position. The shooters alternate from left point to right point. The player in front of the net obscures the goalie's view of the puck.

Make sure your shooters are accurate and keep their shots low. Decrease the time between shots as the drill progresses.

Goalies have legs slightly open, eyes striving to find the puck by looking around the screen. This is a very tough drill that works on reaction to screen shots and helps build mental toughness.

Variation

As your goalies grow adept at this drill, have the point shooters pass the puck back and forth before taking the shot.

Goalie Objective

Goalies must gain optimum position and maintain it as the play continues. They must attempt to "see" the puck at all times.

Screen Shot Drill

S = Shooter
D = Deflector
G = Goalie

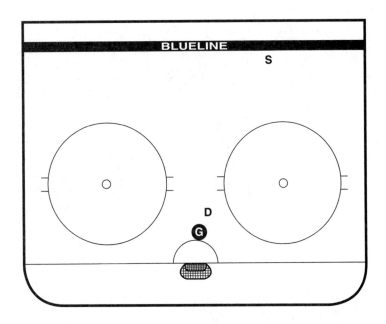

COACH'S JOB

Make sure that goalies understand and employ the three elements of optimum position and that they finish the play. Make sure the shooters keep their shots low.

Note: When the goalie is screened, the normal position from which the screen shot is "heard" is the extended butterfly: stick blade on ice covering Five-Hole, and trapper and blocker extended to cover as much net as possible.

Screen Shot Drill #2

BLIND RECOVERY

PURPOSE
To help goalies practice quickly regaining sight of the puck.

DRILL DESCRIPTION
Position three shooters in a semi-circle in the slot or higher, depending upon the ages and abilities of the goalies. Goalies start in the crease, facing the back boards. On the whistle, goalies turn and pick up the shooter. Have players shoot in a random order, to keep goalies on their toes.

Note: This whole drill works on one whistle (i.e. goalies turn around and shooter shoots).

Goalie Objective
Goalies must quickly find the puck and make the appropriate move to stop the screen shot.

COACH'S JOB
Make sure your goalies find the puck and make the appropriate move. Make sure shots on the goalies are made quickly. There is no point in having the goalies turn and wait for the next shot to arrive. Low shots will require a butterfly position.

Note: If a goalie is turned and waiting for the shot, then the shots are arriving at the net too slowly. In this case, move the shooters closer. Remember — goals and saves are not the objective; reaction and quick movement are the prime concerns. We'd rather see a goalie react well to a fast screen shot than stop a slow one.

Screen Shot Drill #3

BLIND SHOT THROUGH HEAVY TRAFFIC

PURPOSE

Sometimes goalies just can't see the puck. In such cases, they need to listen for the sound of the shot and — when they hear it — drop to the butterfly position.

DRILL DESCRIPTION

You need two players. Have shooter in slot with several pucks. Have the other player right in front of goalie at the top of the crease. Goalies do not try to see the puck — they should hold their head down facing the ice. Shooter slaps the ice once, then shoots. The goalies listen for the first slap, then drop to the butterfly position to cover the entire ice area.

Variation

Move the shooter further out (i.e. to the blueline). Shooter takes shots without first slapping the ice. Goalies listen for the sound of the shot, and immediately regain their feet after the save attempt and once the puck is located. Have shooter shoot quickly, without a lot of time between shots.

Goalie Objective

Goalies must establish optimum position quickly. They must listen carefully and regain feet quickly after save attempt or when puck is located.

COACH'S JOB

Ensure that pads are extended post to post so all the ice is covered; make sure goalies regain feet quickly.

HAND REACTION

When people talk about a goalie having "great reflexes" what they often mean is that the goalie has a quick glove hand. We think of this as a "reflex" reaction, and that there is not much a coach can do to develop reflexes. Studies show, however, that reflexes can be improved through one simple method: practice.

While most of our other drills have an intellectual component, there is not a lot of thought that goes into making a faster glove hand. Goalies just have to face many, many shots to their gloves.

A strategy we like to use is to start off with slow shots in the following drills. Gradually, have the shots become faster — you may need to move the players closer — until the shots are beyond the goalies' capacity to save them. Keep at this level for a while; simply trying to make saves beyond their abilities will help push goalies' reflexes and physical movements to a new level.

There are three drills here. When goalies practice regularly and repeatedly, their reaction times will improve.

Ed Belfour demonstrates his quick glove hand.

Hand Reaction Drill #1

SIMPLE GLOVE SAVES

PURPOSE
To practice both glove hands — the trapper and the blocker.

DRILL DESCRIPTION
Position one shooter in the slot with several pucks. Goalies should be in the crease. Shooter shoots the puck, glove-high, alternating between goalies' trappers and blockers. Have shooters try to get a rhythm going to help the goalies develop a "feel" for the glove saves. As the drill progresses, have shooters shoot faster and harder, trying to score in the top corners.

Goalie Objective
The goalie's key point is to "look" the puck into either glove. This allows better control of the puck, and helps to control the direction of any rebound. Looking ahead depends too much on peripheral vision — the puck can be missed or only partially saved, causing goals or bad rebounds.

COACH'S JOB
See that all the shots are glove-high — no low shots needing butterfly or skate saves. Watch that the goalies eye the puck into glove or blocker.

Note: Don't worry about saves — the repetition forces quickness and concentration.

Hand Reaction Drill #2

LOPSIDED SHOT

PURPOSE

To practice goalies' blocker and trapper hands.

DRILL DESCRIPTION

Position shooter as in Hand Reaction Drill #1. Shooter takes hard shots, aiming for the open net. Increase speed as drill progresses.

The goalies are in the crease, in the half of the crease opposite to the glove hands being drilled. For example, if goalies catch with the right hand, they should stand in the left half of the crease. The idea is to leave a lot of room on the catching side for the shooter to aim at.

Both the blocker and glove should be practiced in a similar manner.

Goalie Objective

Goalies must "look" the puck into the glove and maintain stance. To do this successfully, goalies should drop to one knee with the opposite foot in a T-position, extending the foot with the save attempt.

COACH'S JOB

Again, watch for the shots to be off the ground and well-positioned, and for the goalies to "look" the puck into the glove. After a few times, this drill can be practiced unsupervised.

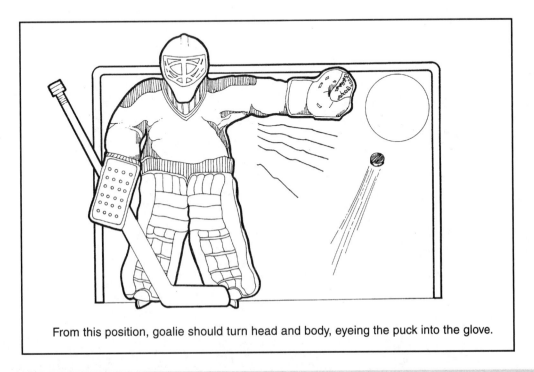

From this position, goalie should turn head and body, eyeing the puck into the glove.

Hand Reaction Drill #3

RAPID FIRE

PURPOSE

To practice goalies' glove hands.

DESCRIPTION

Have players form a semi-circle around the hash mark level. Players each have as many pucks as possible. On your whistle, players take glove-high wrist shots in turn. Goalies should stay deep in crease to force glove movement.

Decrease time between shots as the drill progresses.

Goalie Objective

Goalies must maintain stance while attempting to make the glove saves. Goalies must always "look" the puck into the glove.

COACH'S JOB

Make sure goalies maintain stance and "look" the shots into the glove. Be sure the shooters fire accurate wrist shots.

THE FIVE-HOLE

No part of the goalie's game is more misunderstood by the layperson than the Five-Hole. That's the open area between a goalie's legs. We are tired of hearing TV commentators say that a goalie let in a "soft" goal just because it was scored through the legs. Like the corners, the Five-Hole is a weak spot for any goalie.

As we mentioned earlier, we favour the Inverted-V Style of play. This leaves the legs further apart than in the old-fashioned stand-up style. The result is that the Five-Hole is more vulnerable in the Inverted-V Style, but the bottom corners are better protected.

Kelly Hrudey using the Inverted-V style of play.

Five-Hole Drill #1

BUTTERFLY DROP, WITHOUT STICK

PURPOSE

To help goalies work on protecting the Five-Hole; in particular, to practice going down into the butterfly then recovering quickly.

DRILL DESCRIPTION

Position one shooter in the slot with several pucks. The shooter takes a succession of shots, aiming for the Five-Hole. Gradually increase the speed of the shots, so that goalies are forced to move faster.

Goalies stand at the top of crease, without their sticks. This forces their knees together quickly. They drop to the butterfly to make the save, then quickly regain their feet.

Variation

Add another shooter and alternate shots. Each time, wait till the goalie is set before shooting.

Goalie Objective

Goalies must drop into the butterfly, and then quickly regain feet; goalies must reduce the Five-Hole space as quickly as possible.

COACH'S JOB

Watch for the proper butterfly and for goalies to regain their feet quickly.

Five-Hole Drill #2

BUTTERFLY DROP, WITH STICK

PURPOSE
To help the goalie work on protecting the Five-Hole; in particular, to practice going down into the butterfly, then recovering quickly.

DESCRIPTION
Position shooter as in Five-Hole Drill #1. Goalies stand at the top of crease, using their sticks. They drop to the butterfly to make the save, then quickly regain their feet.

Variation
Add one shooter to the slot, and have them alternate shots to the Five-Hole, as in the previous drill.

Goalie Objective
Goalies must drop into butterfly with stick drawn to knees; goalies must quickly regain feet.

COACH'S JOB
Watch for proper butterfly and for goalies to regain feet right away. Because the goalies now have their sticks, very few goals should go through the Five-Hole.

Five-Hole Drill #3

WITH ANGLE MOTION

PURPOSE

To practice defending the Five-Hole, with players cutting across the front of the net.

DRILL DESCRIPTION

Skaters form rows on each side of the blueline. On your whistle, one skater moves down the wing, then deep cuts in front of the goal. Skaters aim to put the puck between goalies' Five-Holes as they cut across. On your whistle, goalies move quickly to ready position. They follow the skaters as they cut across the net. Goalies use T-Push (see "Skating Drills") to move laterally, remembering to drop the back knee slightly to protect the Five-Hole.

Alternate sides. Quicker whistles force goalies to move faster.

Goalie Objective

Goalies must maintain stance, then do the proper T-Push.

COACH'S JOB

Watch that the goalies drop the back knee slightly during T-Push, to cover the Five-Hole.

Five-Hole Drill #4

DIRECT SHOT WITH MOTION

PURPOSE
To practice defending the Five-Hole when dealing with a direct shot with motion.

DRILL DESCRIPTION
Skaters form one row at the blueline, in line with the goal. On the whistle, a shooter skates straight towards the goal, shooting low at the Five-Hole. Goalies start well out of the crease, then move backwards. They drop to their knees in butterfly to stop-save, stick in front protecting the Five-Hole.

Goalie Objective
Goalies must quickly move to ready position while maintaining stance and backward motion. Goalies should drop to knees with stick on ice snug against knees, so there is no Five-Hole opening.

COACH'S JOB
Watch that the shots are hard, low and accurate. Make sure goalie keeps stick snug to knees, preventing Five-Hole opening.

Five-Hole Drill:
Direct Shot with Motion

S = Shooter
G = Goalie
SP = Starting Point
FP = Finishing Point

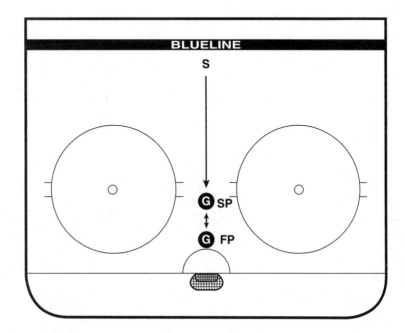

BREAKAWAYS

Breakaways are the most exciting play in hockey. They are also the part of practice that players enjoy the most. Skating is the goalie's key to effectively playing the breakaway. The better a goalie's lateral and vertical motion, the better the chance of making a save.

It's important that goalies move out of the net quickly as a breakaway develops. They must move to the ready position and establish a smooth, steady backwards motion. Timing is important — goalies don't want to be caught in the back of their nets. It's also important that they stay on their feet as long as possible.

Breakaway Drill #1

WITH MOTION

PURPOSE

To improve goalies' ability to follow the play in a breakaway situation. This drill focuses on goalies' forward and backward skating, as well as maintaining proper angle.

DRILL DESCRIPTION

Shooters line up at centre ice. On your whistle, one at a time, they break in on the goalies; they may shoot or deke.

Goalies start in crease. On the whistle, goalies move out to the "ready" position, 10 feet in front of the crease. Instruct them to slowly move backwards as the shooter approaches. They want to make the save before they are in the crease. On a deke, goalies should use backward motion to flow to the post from just inside the crease. On the whistle, they quickly make their way 10 feet beyond the crease again, to face the next shooter. The whistle signifies the next shooter should start — this forces goalies out quickly.

Goalie Objective

Goalies must come out quickly, and then move backwards slowly and smoothly, maintaining proper stance. On the save or goal, goalies should immediately return to the "ready" position — the shooter is coming in on the whistle regardless of where the goalie is positioned.

COACH'S JOB

Watch that goalies maintain proper stance. Also, make sure goalies don't "cheat" by staying too close to the net — they should quickly move at least 10 feet beyond the crease. It is also important that a coach notice breakaway goals that often occur at the same spot (e.g. always low to the stick side).

Breakaway Drill #2

LATERAL MOTION

PURPOSE

To improve goalies' ability to follow the play as it moves from side to side across the ice, and to encourage goalies to use the T-Push.

DRILL DESCRIPTION

Shooters line up on the blueline, on right or left side. On the whistle, they skate down one wing, then cut across to the opposite hash marks. They may shoot any time as they cut across.

Goalies start in crease. On the whistle, they come at least 10 feet out of their crease, to the "ready" position. They follow the shooters cutting across the net, always maintaining a gradual backwards motion, before moving laterally (shuffle procedure). A proper centre line angle is important throughout the drill. Alternate wings.

Goalie Objective

Goalies must come out quickly, and then move sideways quickly and smoothly, maintaining proper stance and angle. Goalies must be in the middle of a line between the puck and the centre of the crossbar. (See "Telescoping," page 29 in Part 1.) It is very important that goalies remain on their feet as they move sideways and make the save. On the whistle goalies must quickly regain the "ready" position, 10 feet outside the crease, preparing for the next shooter.

COACH'S JOB

Watch that goalies maintain proper stance and relative stance, and hold their feet across the crease.

Note: For lateral motion when the play is close to the net, goalies should always use the T-Push style of skating.

Breakaway Drill #3

PENALTY SHOT CHALLENGE

PURPOSE

This drill is a favourite of all players. It's designed to help the goalies cope with a random range of breakaway situations.

DESCRIPTION

Players start at centre ice with one puck. They move in on goalies as if in a penalty shot situation, starting with the puck at centre ice. Players are free to try and score any way they want.

Goalies come well out from their net and assume the ready position. After the skater crosses the blueline, goalies start their steady, smooth backwards motion.

If a player scores, that player gets to try again after everyone else has had a turn. Players keep trying until, through a process of elimination, only one player is left to shoot.

Normally, this game is a no-win situation for the goalies, as the last shooter to score a goal is always declared "winner." We add one little kick at the end, to make things more fair for goalies. The last player has one final shot on goal — if the player scores, then he or she is declared "winner"; if not, the goalie wins.

Goalie Objective

Goalies must quickly establish ready position and smooth backward motion. Goalies must not fall for the fake, and must not go down early. And above all, goalies must concentrate on the puck.

COACH'S JOB

Make sure that goalies establish position and motion. This exercise can be the coach's break — enjoy this fun drill.

TWO-ON-ONE

DEFINITION
A two-on-one occurs when two offensive players come in on one defensive player and the goalie.

TEAM STRATEGY
The defenceman plays in front of, and halfway between, the puck carrier and the other forward as they cross the blueline — he wants to take away the puck carrier's pass option. The defenceman slows down to avoid backing into his goalie while the forwards continue their drive to the net. At some point the pass becomes impossible — the defenceman will be positioned between the puck and the winger. When the pass option is eliminated, the goalie focuses on the shooter.

Goalies are responsible for the puck carrier. In many ways this situation can be played like a breakaway, although the goalies have a much greater advantage here since the amount of ice available to the puck carrier is limited by the presence of the defensive player. If the puck carrier drives to the net, goalies still play the puck and should be assisted by the defenceman. Above all, goalies take the shooter when the pass is no longer possible.

How the System Breaks Down
The system breaks down when defensive players forget their role. They are not there to stop the shot; they are there to take away the pass option from the puck carrier. On the other hand, they do not simply cover the open player — they don't want to take themselves out of the play, leaving open ice for the puck carrier.

There can also be a problem if goalies are not aware of their role. They must concentrate on the puck carrier, and rely on the defensive players to do their job with the open player.

Two-On-One Drill

PURPOSE
To practice a full two-on-one.

DRILL DESCRIPTION
Start with goalies in net, defensive player at the blueline and forwards at the red line. On your whistle the goalies move out of the crease and the two forwards cross the blueline with the puck, with the defenceman positioned in the middle. The defensive player plays the pass and the goalies play the puck. Once he or she hits the face-off circle, the puck carrier may shoot or pass to the open player. The open player must shoot right away, or drive to the net.

Have the second goalie stand at the boards to observe:

- At what point is the pass taken away (i.e. is no pass possible)?
- Did the goalie play the shooter at the right moment?
- Did the goalie stay high?

Variation
Start off slowly until every player knows their role. Increase speed. Make sure puck comes in from both sides of the ice. Allow no more than three passes. Forwards can criss-cross as another variation to this drill.

Goalie Objective
Goalies must quickly gain the ready position, and stay aligned with the puck carrier, keeping focused on the puck.

Two-On-One Drill

F = Forward
D = Defence
G = Goalie

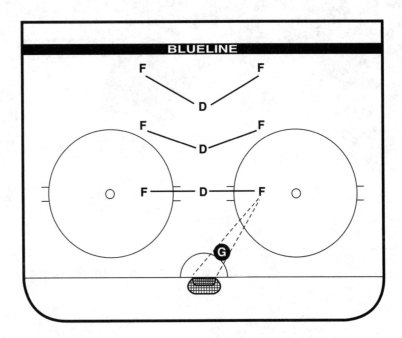

COACH'S JOB

This is a defensive drill, not a passing practice. Encourage vocal communication between the goalie and the defensive player. Make sure that the defence player takes away the pass.

Note: At the point where the two forwards and the defence are even, the pass option is taken away, and the goalie concentrates on the shooter alone.

Bill Ranford communicates with his teammates.

A FEW THOUGHTS ON TEAM PLAY
How Do Goalies Fit Into Team Play?

Goalies are part of a team. They are rarely alone — even on a breakaway or penalty shot, goalies do not bear sole responsibility for the team. Only through a breakdown in the team system do goalies wind up facing shooters one-on-one.

Goalies share a common aim with all the skaters on their team — to keep the puck out of the net. Whenever the opposing team has the puck in the defensive zone, all six players on the defensive team must work as a unit. (Note that the defending team always has a player advantage in an "even-strength" situation — or have you forgotten the goalie already?)

The key to defensive success is communication. When the puck is in the defensive zone, goalies become the focal point of the team; skaters work to take the puck away from the offensive team so that they do not get a shot, or to maximize their goalies' capacity to make a save. To meet this second aim, the skaters must work together on a three-point strategy:

1. Provide a clear view of the puck for the goalie.
2. Provide maximum reaction time for the goalie; that is, the further out the shot, the better.
3. Ensure that a puck play is complete; that is, the puck is either held for a whistle or moved to a safe area of the ice.

How does this system break down?
Well, it's not when the puck goes into the net. A goalie might misplay a shot. But just as often, a team makes a mistake before a shot is even taken. The common mistakes are:

• Players don't take their checks. The result is an open offensive player and often a close-range shot.

• One defensive player tries to cover for another player's mistake. The result: instead of one player out of position, there are two. Two wrongs don't make a right, not even in hockey. Your goalies have a much better chance facing a shooter one-to-one if they know that there is no one left uncovered for the puck carrier to pass to.

• A defensive player decides to play goalie. Too often, a defensive player will park somewhere between the shooter and the goalie, and assume a stance that looks like a cross between a flamingo and a goaltender. This achieves one thing: it reduces the goalie's view of the puck, which means that their chance of making the save is reduced. A defensive player must either skate directly towards the puck shooter, or clear out of the way if they don't want to get hit by the puck.

The key to sound defensive team play is communication. The coach must make sure that all players know their roles, and stick to them. Even in practice, players should be talking to each other all the time.

CONCLUSION
It's Up To You

In Part 1 of *Behind The Mask*, we stressed that having proper stance, angles and motion were the cornerstones of proper goaltending. Weakness in any one area will severely inhibit a goalie's progress. It is simple: if you can't skate, or aren't able to retain proper stance and angles, you'll find game situations — breakaways, two-on-ones — next to impossible.

In Part 2 of this book, the essence of drill technique is repetition and high-tempo execution. Time and time again, we stress that we're looking for improved speed and technique, not saves. For example, if a shot is at 80 kilometres per hour, the goalie is conditioned to match that pace. If a shot is at 110 kilometres per hour, we know the goalie may not make the save, but we also know that the goalie is moving in excess of 80 kilometres per hour — perhaps at 90 to 100 kilometres per hour. This is essential to a goalie's development; the saves will come later.

While there can be a variety of drills for any one purpose, the ultimate secret in training goalies is to push them to a level previously thought to be unachievable. In Part 2, we have continued to advocate for the goaltending basics of skating, angles and stance, but at a progressively higher level. We have come full circle in the development of today's young goaltenders. Now, it truly is up to you.

About the Authors

Chris Gudgeon is a former house goalie and bestselling author, whose books include *An Unfinished Conversation: The Life and Music of Stan Rogers*, *Out of This World: The Natural History of Milton Acorn*, and *Consider the Fish: Fishing for Canada From Campbell River to Petty Harbour*. He is married to author Barbara Stewart, whose recently revised and updated *She Shoots, She Scores* was the first-ever hockey book just for girls. They live in Victoria, British Columbia, with their three sons.

Ian Young is a professional goaltending consultant. A teammate of Bobby Orr in the mid-1960s, he was drafted by the Boston Bruins and headed for an NHL career when an errant slapshot blinded him in one eye. He is currently president of the Goal-Pro Group Ltd., a company dedicated to providing skill development for goalies.

BRIGHT LIGHTS FROM POLESTAR BOOK PUBLISHERS

Polestar Book Publishers takes pride in creating books that enrich our understanding of the world and introducing discriminating readers to exciting writers. We publish fiction, poetry, teen fiction and non-fiction in a variety of areas. Here are some of our best-selling sports titles.

Amazing Allstar Hockey Activity Book *by Jesse, Noah and Julian Ross*
Terrific trivia, awesome quizzes, radical stats, action photos, weird hockey history and a lot more — hours of hands-on fun for young hockey fans.
1-896095-92-5 • $5.95 Can • $4.95 US

Celebrating Excellence: Canadian Women Athletes *by Wendy Long*
A collection of biographical essays and photos that showcases more than 200 athletes who have achieved excellence.
1-896095-04-6 • $29.95 Can • $24.95 US

Get the Edge: Audrey Bakewell's Power SkatingTechnique *by Audrey Bakewell*
Skating specialist Audrey Bakewell provides basic and advanced drills for power skating, a skill fundamental to the game of hockey.
1-896095-21-6 • $18.95 Can • $16.95 US

Home Run: A Modern Approach to Baseball Skill Building *by Michael McRae*
Skills specialist McRae offers a solid base of technical instruction for players and coaches who are learning and teaching baseball fundamentals.
$18.95 Can/$15.95 USA

Long Shot: Steve Nash's Journey to the NBA *by Jeff Rud*
Profile of young NBA star Steve Nash, detailing the determination and skill that carried him through high school and college basketball into the ranks of the pros.
1-896095-16-X • $18.95 Can • $16.95 US

Our Game: A Collection of All-Star Hockey Fiction *by Doug Beardsley, editor*
From the Forum to the backyard rink, this collection of 30 stories illuminates the essence of the hockey soul.
1-896095-32-1 • $18.95 Can • $16.95 US

Thru the Smoky End Boards: Canadian Poetry About Sports and Games *by Kevin & Sean Brooks, ed.*
More than 70 poets celebrate the glory of sport, and examine not only the athlete and the fan, but also the anti-fan and the skeptic. Poems about hockey, baseball, football, basketball, swimming and more.
1-896095-15-1 • $16.95 Can • $14.95 US

Too Many Men on the Ice: Women's Hockey in North America *by Joanna Avery and Julie Stevens*
A fascinating look at all levels of women's hockey in Canada and the United States, including in-depth profiles of prominent players.
1-896095-33-X • $19.95 Can • $16.95 US

Polestar titles are available from your local bookseller. For a copy of our complete catalogue, send a 8.5x11 SASE to:

Polestar Book Publishers
PO Box 5238, Station B
Victoria, BC
Canada   V8R 6N4
http://mypage.direct.ca/p/polestar